D0858359

Unwin Education Books: 35 22-7

THE PLACE OF COMMONSENSE IN
EDUCATIONAL THOUGHT

Unwin Education Books

Series Editor: Ivor Morrish, BD, BA, Dip.Ed(London), BA(Bristol)

Unwin Education Books: 35
Series Editor : Ivor Morrish

The Place of Commonsense in Educational Thought

(Herbert)

LIONEL ELVIN
Emeritus Professor of Education, University of London

London
GEORGE ALLEN & UNWIN LTD
RUSKIN HOUSE   MUSEUM STREET

First published in 1977

ISBN 0 04 370078 0 hardback
      0 04 370079 9 paperback

Printed in Great Britain in 10 on 11 point Times Roman
by Cox & Wyman Ltd, London, Fakenham and Reading

Foreword

Anyone who gives a book the kind of title I have given immediately exposes himself to two charges. The first is that he thinks himself to be full of commonsense and that those he takes issue with, and indeed other people in general, are not. I trust that I may be acquitted of such arrogance. But if a man does think that good sense leads to a certain conclusion he must say so, and say why. If others can bring better sense to bear on the other side of an argument then he must accept it. Till then he must make his case and put what he thinks to be his sensible cards on the table.

Secondly, such a writer is likely to be charged with supposing that commonsense will solve every problem and that more specialist study and more highly theoretical work are not necessary. I do not take this view at all. In my own career I have benefited immensely from the friendship, counsel and teaching of more specialist colleagues. At the same time I have found, first as director of the education department of Unesco and then as director of the Institute of Education of the University of London, that apart from such reading as I could do myself in specialist fields I had in the end to rely on what I hope was informed commonsense in coming to conclusions, whether as to advice to give on this or that line of policy or as part of my own thinking about education. Most teachers and student teachers, most administrators, and indeed the interested public are in very much this sort of position and, while learning what they can from the experts, have to see what their own commonsense can do to guide them to sound decisions. That is the exercise I have set myself in this work. I would ask the reader to note that the title I have chosen is not *Commonsense in Education* – that would suggest a familiar kind of no-nonsense obtuseness that I trust is not mine – but *The Place of Commonsense in Educational Thought*. The different emphasis is deliberate. Indeed, in one chapter I point out that one kind of supposed commonsense, the kind that instead of thinking something out merely seeks a comfortable halfway house, will not do.

There is no need, I hope, to undertake an elaborate commentary on the word 'commonsense'. As with most terms there are difficulties about it, but its general bearing is well enough understood. What I have chiefly in mind is the capacity to consider an idea or a proposal in the light of the lessons of non-specialised experience. Thus, if a single school were invited to be the vehicle of three large-scale experiments at once, each of which was backed by its appropriate experts and all of which seemed worthwhile, the headmaster would almost certainly say: 'Yes, but how many major disruptions can a school stand at one and the same time? I'll undertake one, but not all three at once.' This would be the voice of commonsense, not quarrelling with the professional proposals as such, but saying that a patient cannot undergo too many major operations at the same time and survive.

Commonsense criticism of theories is more difficult to evaluate. It may come out of traditional views, and these may be relevant and sound, or not so. If there is blank refusal to look at new ways of conceiving a question on grounds of supposed commonsense, that is normally prejudice. If the theory is a hypothesis subsuming evidence, then it cannot be rejected by mere commonsense. It must be tested against the evidence. But we cannot test every theory, however wild. It is reasonable to expect the innovator to provide grounds for judging whether on the face of it there is something to examine further.

Science was once described as applied commonsense. If scientists just continued to 'apply' commonsense there would be little scientific discovery. This often comes about by apparently defying commonsense. But when a discovery has been vindicated it enters into the commonsense of the next generation and seems only to be commonsense carried further. It was long obvious to commonsense that the earth was flat. Yet commonsense had not gone far enough, for as the familiar school illustration shows, you have only to see that the funnels of a ship are still visible when the hull has disappeared over the horizon for commonsense to tell you that the surface of the earth must be curved. We often do not see what is under our eyes until there has been an imaginative leap, and that rarely comes from the merely commonsense person.

On the other hand, as we all know, the logical development of an idea may outrun sound judgement. The man who is heady with it may see things that the ordinary person does not see, but equally he may not see what the ordinary person can see very plainly. The astronomer out for a night walk and gazing intently at the stars did fall into the well. In so practically important a matter as education there must always be an appeal to experience. It is the part of prejudice on either side to refuse it. The refusal may lie with the self-styled practical man, such as the experienced teacher who learned all there was to learn about education a long time ago, or with a theorist gone doctrinaire who does not sufficiently allow the validity of practical reason. Of course the assumptions of commonsense have to be challenged. People who say they 'take their stand on principle' and who singularly fail to explain what their principle is and the reasons for it, are to be held suspect; and those who take their stand on unexplained commonsense no less so. But it is also possible to move with great skill through abstractions and seem to be reasoning in what is nearly a vacuum. The distinction I would make is not between the man of commonsense and the man who follows reasoning, but between the man of commonsense and the man who reasons about education within too narrow a framework of reference.

This is the essence of my 'commonsense' criticism of those I criticise in the following pages, whether they be curriculum theorists who press a single approach too far, teachers of classics who are reluctant to adapt to a changed educational scene, defenders of compulsory religious education who have not realised that the relevant question is not about religion but about fairness in a multi-belief society, research workers who will not consider the setting in which their findings will be received, or philosophers, teachers and administrators who will not see that theirs is not the only voice in what must be a general conversation. Commonsense is not to be confused with prejudice, though prejudice claims to appeal to it. But neither is it to be dismissed as coming from people who are not initiated into this or that 'mystery' (I use the word in its mediaeval sense), as those who want to use it too often feel it may be.

It is this prevailing attitude, or theme, that gives this book its unity. It may be argued that a specialist who forms a hypothesis should run it for all it is worth and exploit every possibility of fruitfulness until evidence and criticism persuade him to modify or even abandon it. But the rest of us must come to a balanced judgement in the face of rival theories and rival policy proposals. I argue that, in doing this, informed commonsense is not an inferior substitute for real grounds of opinion but an essential ingredient.

To illustrate such a theme many examples of educational thinking might be used. I have chosen some in which I have been especially interested and on which I have lectured or written over the years. I have not tried to write a comprehensive, but an illustrative, book on the subject: I hope a reasonably convincing one.

My debt to those with whom I have talked education over many years is very great. To particularise may be a little invidious but I should like to say how much I have owed especially to my former colleagues Professor Richard Peters and Professor W. D. Wall, with whom (as may be seen here and there in the following pages) I enjoy the occasional difference of view almost as much as our normal agreement. I would like also to thank my son, Dr Mark Elvin, who suggested the theme of this book after reading a few of my papers. And the staff of the London Institute of Education Library have left me in their debt, as they have so many others, for their helpfulness and skill in locating books and periodicals.

I would also like to thank the following for permission to use material they have published: Allen & Unwin for the use in Chapter 4 of a substantial part of my paper in *Religious Education, 1944–1984* (1966); the National Institute of Adult Education for the use in part in Chapter 6 of an article I wrote for *Adult Education* (December 1947); the Melbourne University Press for permission to draw in Chapter 7 on a paper in *Melbourne Studies in Education, 1968–69*; and the *Oxford Review of Education* for permission to reprint as Chapter 10 an article I wrote for Vol. I, No. 3 (1975).

Finally, as some of these chapters had their first airing in lectures in the School of Teacher Education of the Canberra College of Advanced Education, in 1974, and Chapter 1 in a paper read at the Headmasters' Conference in Perth in 1975, I would like to thank my friends and colleagues in Australia for the opportunities they gave me to study there, and not least for their generous hospitality to my wife and myself while we were their guests.

H. L. E.
February 1976

Contents

Böcke, zur Linken mit euch! so ordnet künftig der Richter:
Und ihr Schäfchen, ihr sollt ruhig zur Rechten mir stehn!
Wohl! Doch eines ist noch von ihm zu hoffen; dann sagt er:
Seid, Vernünftige, mir grad gegenüber gestellt!

Goethe: 'Venezianische Epigramme'[1]

PART 1 COMMONSENSE AND THE CURRICULUM

Chapter 1

Curriculum Theory and Curriculum Reform

The simple idea of a school is that it is a place to which children go to learn things that they could not so conveniently learn except in a special place and with special teachers. What they are taught there (though not exactly the same as what they may learn there) is therefore a quite central question. It has to be thought about. This brings into play general ideas about education, learning and teaching, and when a certain point of conscious refinement in such thinking is reached we begin to speak of curriculum theory. There has been a considerable effort to develop curriculum theory in recent years, and although this is to be welcomed one can hardly be happy with some of the results. A good deal of it does not stand up to the tests of commonsense, and because I cannot believe that commonsense tests are to be ruled out of court, and because this is so central a matter, I would like to start with an examination of some of this thinking about the curriculum, pausing later in this part of this book to look at two difficult particular subject problems.

It will already be evident that by the curriculum of a school (or college or university) I mean simply its organised programme of studies and activities. I am aware that some contemporary writers would consider this too narrow a definition, and I will take up that point later. Meanwhile, since it is what people have had in mind till now by the term it seems to me to avoid certain confusions, I retain it.

Now if only because times and needs change, thoughtful people are bound to ask whether a prevailing curriculum is the most appropriate one. But what are the criteria for deciding what is appropriate? One criterion is the needs of children and young people, as they show them (for instance by interest or boredom) and as we try to judge them. Another criterion is the needs of our society in the immediate future and also more permanently. These two tests are not necessarily antithetical. Most young people want to fit into society, whatever their protest about this or that feature of it, and there is a large area where their needs and those of society overlap. But the overlap is not complete, and the approaches differ. I would say that either without the other is useless, but because in the educational thinking of the last fifty years or so there has been rather more emphasis on the first I am inclined to bring the second more into the discussion.

However, some theorists of the curriculum reject both these criteria as major determinants of what should be taught in schools. They say that we should plan the curriculum on prior principles, on a comprehensive theory of what a curriculum should be, and reject these two criteria as too pragmatic. The proposal that we should think out our principles first and then make a plan accordingly always seems logical and attractive. In general there is too little educational theory rather than too much, too little of an attempt to examine whether what we do is justified and too little examination of the concepts that we use. Nevertheless it seems to me that the urge to formulate comprehensive theories about the curriculum has been premature and has produced theories that run counter to critical good sense. For this reason, before discussing curriculum reform in more pragmatic terms, related to the first two criteria I have mentioned, I shall consider this third approach to the planning of the curriculum and explain why it has led to conclusions that at any rate to me seem unsatisfactory.

Whether this be so or not, such theoretical thinking has at least prodded us to ask whether we have got our curricular balance right at the present time. There is normally a bad time-lag between the schools and social needs and we must try to guard against this. For instance, long after what we call the Renaissance in the West, schools and universities were still teaching mediaeval matter in a mediaeval way. I think our conservatism is not quite as supine as that. I like the phrase of an American writer quoted by Professor Hoyle,[1] that the readiness of a school to consider innovations is a sign of its organisational health.

As we think more about what we are doing we begin to formulate general ideas, and to that extent to think theoretically. Yet theory is rather a high word. You don't come by comprehensive theories easily, and to formulate one prematurely may be merely to rationalise a bias. I would say that this happened in the study of educational administration in the United States. With an unwise haste to give this complicated field of study a theoretical basis they borrowed heavily from the theory of business administration. As a result Professor Halpin,[2] then of Chicago, had to get together a book of essays whose purpose, in part, was to explain to superintendents of schools that schools and factories were different. Those of us who had not been victims of such theorising might have been trusted to take this for granted.

Something of the same kind has been happening in curriculum study. Professor Lawton[3] is modest in his theoretical claims. He is searching for relevant general factors in the study of the curriculum, yet he uses the word 'theory' sparingly. But he is rather an exception. Professor Whitfield[4] and others cry out that what we need above all to get our practice right is a good curriculum theory. It seems to me that in the present state of the art the formulation of supposedly comprehensive theories is more likely to distort than to illuminate. Let me give three examples. They all begin with an idea that has something to it. They are all developed by educationists of standing. And they are all vitiated by trying to be too general, too comprehensive, inviting a kind of rigidity in both theory and practice.

Professor Benjamin Bloom and his colleagues who drew up that 'taxonomy' of educational objectives[5] began with the painful discovery that people setting examinations and devising curricula did not have a clear idea as to what their objectives were. What were they examining for? What exactly were they trying to teach, and what exactly were they expecting their pupils to learn? To press these questions was laudable. For years in this country examining bodies have not faced the question, or have failed to act on any answer, as to whether with one and the same examination you can both test the average candidate's past performance and pick out the exceptionally good who may be expected to do well in three years at the university. Again, the tangles of alleged reasons for teaching this or that subject, or for marked specialisation in the sixth form, are only now beginning to be sorted out – some reasons looking reputable and others being little more than folklore. If Bloom and his colleagues prodded people into thinking these things out, well and good, though one may doubt whether the immense apparatus of meetings and conferences and of exchange of papers they got involved in was necessary to get sensible answers.

Unfortunately they made it their purpose to analyse teaching and curriculum making in terms of what they called behavioural objectives, and this is not an adequate basis for thinking about what we do in education. Now disillusionment has set in. The *OECD Handbook on Curriculum Development*[6] describes this disillusionment with curriculum planning based on behavioural objectives. 'Education,' it says, 'cannot be viewed as just an applied science. If there must be a scientific metaphor, better the gradual adaptation of organisms over evolutionary history than one that derives from armies and war industry. But judgement and values must enter into curricular, as all educational decisions.'

Bloom, then, is concerned with 'educational objectives defined in behavioural terms'. He is not here concerned with what is worth learning or worth teaching. He classifies his objectives without discussing whether they are good objectives. 'It was further agreed,' he says, 'that in constructing the taxonomy every effort should be made to avoid value judgements about objectives or behaviours.' This no doubt gives the work the air of value-free science. But neither teachers nor parents can avoid the question: should we encourage this, or discourage that, in a developing child? It is a question, as Mr Macdonald-Ross says in an admirable article,[7] that just will not go away. You must ask what constitutes a good education. The Bloom recipe relates to performance. Yet the results of tests and examinations are not the same thing as education. Bloom does ask us to ask what we are testing for. He does not ask why we think it important to test for it at all.

It is true that this whole procedure comes from experience of training in the army and war industry, not from education. (Theirs not to reason why; theirs but to train and die.) To break down every period into little 'objectives' of teaching time may be a good way of teaching certain skills, including some that should be learned at school, but it is not education. The general objection is well put by Professor Chomsky:

There are strong pressures to make use of new educational technology and to design curriculum and teaching methods in the light of the latest scientific advances. In itself, this is not objectionable. It is important, nevertheless, to remain alert to a very real danger: that new knowledge and technique will define the nature of what is taught and how it is taught, rather than contribute to the realisation of educational goals that are set on other grounds, and in other terms. Let me be concrete. Technique and even technology is available for rapid and efficient inculcation of skilled behaviour, in language teaching, teaching of arithmetic and other domains. There is, consequently, a real temptation to reconstruct curriculum in the terms defined by the new technology. And it is not too difficult to invent a rationale, making use of the concepts of 'controlling behaviour', enhancing skills, and so on. Nor is it difficult to construct objective tests that are sure to demonstrate the effectiveness of such methods in reaching certain goals that are incorporated in these tests. But successes of this sort will not demonstrate that it is important to concentrate on developing skilled behaviour in the student. What little we know about human intelligence would at least suggest something quite different: that by diminishing the range and complexity of materials presented to the inquiring mind, by setting behaviour in fixed patterns, these methods may harm and distort the normal development of creative abilities.[8]

The theory on which Chomsky is commenting mixes up curriculum making and teaching methods, and my preference for an older definition of curriculum is therefore relevant here. If curriculum and method had been kept distinct in the minds of Professor Bloom and his colleagues when they came to the curriculum they would have had to ask themselves why we include this or that in it and so to have realised that value judgements must come in.

The case against their teaching methods is no less strong. This kind of scheme imprisons the teacher. It atomises experiences that cannot be chopped up into little bits. As Miss Sarah Moskovitz has pointed out,[9] it makes the teacher an interchangeable part in a mechanical process instead of a creative agent, and for the pupils denies the whole liberating effect of their creative participation in what is going on.

Teaching is a living art, not a dead drill. Naturally teaching and learning should have a framework, but everything is not 'set' as a machine is set to perform a given operation. Anything may come up. The teacher should have an assured understanding of what it means to be an educated person but then infinite adaptability to different situations and human beings. How can this 'taxonomy' help a teacher in daily practice? How do you use the twenty-nine itemised objectives under the heading 'Knowledge' in the summary of taxonomy? I would be puzzled to say. Its usefulness has been held to lie in helping us to think out what the elements of knowledge are, and there is something in this. But it is vitiated by the narrow use of the concept, emphasising the remembering in which people can be trained and neglecting something more important, understanding. Bloom says that knowledge as defined in the book includes 'those behaviours and test-situations' that emphasise remembering. But behaviour (I leave aside the unlovely but now sadly modish plural) is not the same as knowledge and cannot be part of its definition. Action may give evidence of the grasp of a concept but it is not the same thing as a concept and cannot be part of it.

It is no answer to say that progress comes because we develop a theory and then modify it as we find that it is not adequate. Some theories do subsume what is known at a given time and are modified as time reveals new data. But we know quite enough already to have given Professor Bloom and his colleagues pause before they went on from their first rueful observation about examiners to a theory that claimed to be much too comprehensive. A study or two on the first pertinent question, yes: but this elaborated overstatement, backed by so much effort and money and gaining so much influence, surely not.

My second example is different, except that once again a pertinent observation has been injudiciously expanded. To be fair to Professor Bantock, he calls his contribution to the Open University book on the curriculum simply 'Towards a Theory'.[10] But this disarming phrase is sometimes used as a defence mechanism (did Professor Bantock have in mind T. S. Eliot's *Notes Towards a Definition of Culture*?, a book whose most inadequately argued theses about society it was thus made to seem almost indelicate to attack?).

The pertinent observation, though a familiar one, is that some children develop the capacity to handle concepts well, while others continue to find them difficult. Bantock is also rightly concerned that the high culture of our civilisation should be transmitted and not overwhelmed by the mediocrity, and worse, of the contemporary demotic scene. This leads him to suggest that there should in general be two kinds of curriculum. One, for the academic, should be book-based. The other should be related to folk culture rather than high culture and should be based on the art of movement and related non-verbal arts. What he means by the first kind of curriculum is readily comprehensible. The recipe for the second I find bizarre. But leaving aside for the moment the difficulty of working out this second kind of curriculum practice, has Bantock thought through the implications for our society of the dualism of curriculum that he recommends? Or has he simply noted the dangers that our high culture runs and then rather thrown off a much too sweeping suggestion? Much as I respect Professor Bantock, I think this is what has taken place.

We are no longer a society of mandarins and peasants. It is no longer a matter of justice only, but of necessity, that everyone should be able to read (which, in the elementary sense, Bantock of course admits) and to read with as much critical awareness as possible. Our young people need to be able to examine the slogans they hear on every side. In politics they will have the vote; in the economy they are consumers that the market cannot ignore; in general society they will contribute, for good or ill, to the quality of all our lives. They need an education based on literacy and the examination of ideas for their own well-being; and society needs a wide generality of such citizens for its well-being.

Even if these objections did not have force there would be the difficulty that proposers of selective schemes tend to gloss over – and have since Plato – unless of course they base their selection not on ability but on inherited wealth and status. How and when do you make your selection for the two different kinds of education? If they are to be radically separate you cannot leave your selection late. But the ability to handle concepts is apt to develop rather late; even ability with words, which may be a useful criterion at the top and the bottom, is not very reliable around the middle because of the difficulty of allowing both for late development and for the influence of home and environment; and there are some able people whose intelligence is not strongly verbal. We have abandoned selection at 11 because even with good tests it was not precise enough even for meritocratic justice, and we are not likely to go back to it now.

Professor Bantock has gone off into his proposal for a double curriculum much too hurriedly. But if it is important to conserve and to deepen our traditions of high culture, how is this to be done? Apart from social policies to counter the forces in our society that make for triviality and the degrada-tion of standards, there would seem to be two educational ways open to us. One is to raise the level of general education, the other is to employ a greater variety of teaching methods in accordance with the needs of the individuals we teach.

The curriculum should have a common basis, with increasing possibility of choice of studies towards the end of the school experience, improving (not, as at present, often running counter to) the prospects of good general education. We have for a good time now got away from the notion that if you wished to be an educated man Latin was indispensable, but we have never thought out clearly for the secondary school what is indispensable and should be common and compulsory and what kinds of variety will make general education 'take' better rather than distort it. We have offered a constricted kind of choice: too often, just a few sciences, or just a few arts subjects, and a great handicap in the sixth form for schools or students who want to bridge this gap.

With the right kind of planned curriculum there should be scope for those who are good at a highly conceptual subject (mathematics being the most obvious example) to go farther and faster than those who are not. But this is very different from Bantock's rigid scheme. Indeed it is difficult to see how his scheme could work out, with conceptual and book-based sub-jects in one curriculum and less conceptual non-book subjects in the other. It is well known that ability in mathematics and music often go together. It might be argued that music is conceptual, but its concepts are not verbal. Since music is not verbal or book-based it would have to fall into Bantock's second class. But the concepts of mathematics are not verbal either, so is mathematics to be excluded from the studies of those who are really academic? The whole proposal breaks down as soon as you try to translate it into an actual curriculum.

Even more fundamentally wrong is the idea, not of a cultivated minority, but of a separated minority culture. Quite simply, this will not work. If things are like that you can be sure that a civilisation is at its last gasp. If high culture is to be vital it must emerge now from a general culture of which it is part. A few individuals in the last days of a civilisation may no doubt withdraw and cultivate their gardens, but the barbarians will soon be at the garden gate. If the masses are barbarians (and I would want to put a lot of qualifications to that statement) there is only one thing to do: to awaken their admiration and respect for the culture they could thought-lessly destroy. Since this cannot now be done by the weight of a tradition that because of their social subordination they just have to accept, how is it to be done? Once again we come back to the relationship between curriculum and methods.

It has often been said that if a boy or girl does not seem apt for a particular study the teacher blames him or her, not himself. It will remain true that some are more apt at some things than at others and some more apt at practically everything than the less fortunate. But much more may be done with these than the routine-minded teacher realises, if methods are made to suit the student, I once head Professor Raymond Aron say that there was no substitute for real culture. So-called pop culture was not. He was right, even if a little rigid. He went on to say that research in France had shown that those who made up the bulk of the audiences at concerts, at good theatre and at lectures, and the bulk of visitors to museums, were those who had been educated at *lycées*. Yes: and the French *lycée*, for all its excellence in its own mode, has been notoriously conservative in its teaching methods. Traditionally its teachers have been virtually untrained except in their matter. Now the traditional *lycée* is crumbling. Upper secondary education has extended greatly and its clientele is no longer simply the highly motivated professional middle class. Faced with a situation for which most of them have been left totally unprepared, the teachers have to think about different methods, and many of them are at a loss. Yet they face an unavoidable imperative.

We can hardly afford to be complacent, though I would say that we are in a somewhat better state. What can be done through real thought about our teaching methods? The most exciting English lesson I have seen (and I take Professor Bantock's key criterion for differentiation, literacy) was in Albert Rowe's then school at Braintree in Essex. Rowe believed that every youngster, bright or not so bright, should be helped to get the best com-mand he could of his own language and that for the less academic the best way in was through the delight everyone feels in finding words to express the experiences he has had through his senses, what he has seen or heard, tasted or even smelt. I watched the vocabulary of a very unacademic class grow. They found words, starting perhaps with one only one boy knew, to describe the appearance and the feeling of two common objects each child had on his desk, a couple of soft drink bottles, one serrated or cor-rugated (they got both these words), the other with a smooth surface. I saw the vocabulary of comprehension turn into vocabulary of use. And they delighted in it because it helped them to realise personal experience. I thought of the English grammar (in fact bogus adaptation from Latin grammar) that I had had at school. I survived, but these boys and girls would not have done so. They did now, because of the use of different and imaginative teaching methods.

Professor Bantock, starting with a concern that no one should dismiss, talked of different curricula when he should have thought of different methods. In the case of Professor Bloom and his colleagues it was a method (and one open to severe criticism) tending to dictate the curriculum, as Chomsky said it would. In the case of Professor Bantock it is wrong-headedness about the curriculum because of too little attention to methods. I remain convinced that while to insist on the relation of the curriculum to methods is important, to consider each in its own right and not to use the word curriculum as a hold-all is a necessary thing in analysis before the synthesis can take place happily in the classroom.

If Professor Bantock suffers from a too little worked-out theory, another writer to whom one listens with attention, Professor Paul Hirst, suffers from one that is too extensively applied. His writings on the philosophy of the curriculum have added to our understanding of some of the problems involved, not in the practical matter of compiling a curriculum – that is not his purpose – but in seeing what we should be thinking about while doing so. All the same I have never been able to accept his thesis that all knowledge is logically locatable within a number of distinct domains (mathematics, the physical sciences, knowledge of persons, literature and the fine arts, morals, religion and philosophy), each of which has its distinct criteria of truth and therefore its distinct form of knowledge.[11] I emphasise that it is the ultra style of this formulation that I find difficult to accept. The milder, more inclusive terms (as not insisting on the cognitive alone), like 'modes of discourse' or Mr Peterson's 'modes of human experience', I find better, embodying the idea of what a curriculum should consist of without forcing on us the cognitive philosopher's frame. Really, when it comes to thinking what a curriculum should be about this extreme and rigid doctrine seems to me to be unnecessary.

To go thoroughly into Professor Hirst's views would entail a lengthy discussion. Here I must at least indicate why I should have preferred his observations as to what we should have in mind when planning a curriculum without the would-be total theory that defeats itself because it leaves out too much.

Hirst does not claim that his forms of knowledge are totally distinct, yet he insists that they are logically distinct, so much so that their criteria as to what is true are special to each and are of fundamentally different kinds. This half-concession to the idea of knowledge that is to some degree common leaves the reader rather baffled, yet for Hirst the differences are clearly much more important than anything in common: 'fundamentally different kinds' is a strong phrase. Are there so many fundamentally different kinds of knowledge? I agree with Mr A. J. Watt of Monash University who says,[12] following Hume, that the one real distinction is between mathematics and other studies. Mathematics relies for its validity on internal consistency alone; other studies involve in addition the test of correspondence with human experience. These are the basic criteria of what knowledge is. Apparent differences are not fundamental but come from the context or the method of inquiry.

Professor Hirst does give some examples of his supposed different kinds in his paper, 'Liberal education and the nature of knowledge' in *Knowledge and the Curriculum*,[13] but they are not analysed so as to give real support to his strong central thesis. Gravity is a concept appropriate to physics and not to history, but that is because the phenomena that lead to it occur in the area of knowledge we call physics. History perplexed Hirst for some time. He says he decided in the end that it is a mixed case, involving on the one hand statements of past fact with their truth criteria and on the other hand explanations of people's actions in terms of their hopes, ambitions, etc. with their different criteria. This won't do at all. A historian, as distinct from a fanciful writer of 'psycho-biography', relies in both cases on the evidence. If he says that Cromwell became a dictator but for a long time hoped to avoid having to assume that role, his second statement must get its warrant from evidence, and the fact that evidence for the first statement is easier to come by does not alter this in the least. The truth criterion is the same in both cases.

The categories that should have perplexed Professor Hirst are those of what he calls knowledge in religion and in the arts. Mr Watt says he finds it obscure by what criteria religion and art came to be included with physical science as a form of *knowledge*; and asks, if our tolerance is to be extended so far, why it should not extend to astrology, or even chess? This is not being facetious. Leaving on one side for the moment the use of the word knowledge, what are the truth criteria for deciding what to accept and what not to accept in the immensely varied propositions made in the world's religions? Presumably many of these Professor Hirst does not accept. I do not know if he believes in Reincarnation or in the Resurrection, but let us assume that he does not accept the former and does accept the latter. What are the criteria by which he rejects the former as true knowledge and accepts the latter? They must not be those of physical science or of history, on his theory. Then what are they, and how do they enable him to make the distinction?

Most people, whether believers or unbelievers, would I think say that in the end acceptance of such beliefs is a matter of faith. (Hirst notes this, but isn't content with it.) If they claim they have knowledge they say that it is revealed knowledge, not knowledge established in the ordinary way. That is the difference that enables believers in a religious proposition to accept it, and equally the reason for its non-acceptance of those who reject it. Hirst says (without formally committing himself to agreement, but strongly implying it) that recent reconsideration of the concept of truth, and the correspondence theory in particular,[14] suggests that the notion of truth is centrally a demand for objective judgement. This is not worked out in relation to religion and the arts, and we are not told what the distinctive truth criteria in these realms are; and the pressure for formal rationality is so strong in Professor Hirst that he keeps coming back to words like objective and propositional, which one instinctively feels are not the right words, or at least the most important words, in these contexts.

This is most clearly evident in the paper 'Literature and the fine arts as a unique form of knowledge'.[15] Professor Hirst must forgive me for saying that I cannot image any poet or artist, or anybody really concerned with poetry and the arts, finding anything in that paper that is remotely related to his studies or creative activities. Logically Professor Hirst must establish that in this realm there is a distinct form of knowledge, one subject to objective criteria, and that this is of cardinal importance for understanding a poem, a picture or a symphony. At least he feels that the cognitive role of the arts (whatever else they may contribute) must first be established if the overall logic of the curriculum is to be soundly developed. In his paper, sensing perhaps that he is not on strong ground, he ends by saying that whether there are objective judgements here he is not in a position to decide, but he thinks the case should be carefully considered. Unfortunately he must be in a position to decide. His theory falls to the ground if he cannot justify the claim that the arts do constitute a special 'form of knowledge' of a cognitive, propositional kind. For this is one of his essential 'forms', and if you leave it out you leave out a major part of any curriculum.

We are of course speaking, as Hirst makes clear, not of knowledge in the sense of familiarity with, nor of technical knowledge (knowing how), but of propositional knowledge (knowing that). Now this may seem to be present in some poetry, especially of the didactic kind, but it is surely not the point of poetry or the arts at all. When we have heard a quartet of Haydn's we do not say, 'That has taught me several important true propositions'. We say we have had a musical experience of great value and delight. This can be accommodated within phrases like 'modes of experience' or 'modes of discourse'. It is outside the formula 'forms of knowledge'. That is why, with regret, I part company with Professor Hirst.

If we are considering the principles of planning a curriculum this is of great importance. Professor Hirst agrees that there may be other legitimate purposes in education besides those he mentions, such as practical training of one kind or another, and the education of character. He recognises that some studies may do things outside the framework of his discourse. Poetry, for instance, may give delight. The liberal education he describes is not claimed to be a total good education, nor can it be just equated with general education; but he maintains that it does draw together those elements in a total education that are logically basic. This seems to me quite wrong-headed. And for two reasons.

Professor Hirst seems to me always to have overemphasised the cognitive side of education. Of fundamental importance though it is, it is not the only fundamentally important function of education as it has been understood in human society. In his paper 'Liberal education and the nature of knowledge' Professor Hirst says that the fully developed Greek notion of liberal education was rooted in a number of philosophical doctrines about knowledge and the relation of knowledge to reality, and this was how the Greeks attained their notion of liberal education. One gets a little tired of the indiscriminate term, 'the Greeks': there were more Greeks than those who lived in Athens and more living in Athens than Socrates, Plato and Aristotle. If one can generalise about Greek education, from Homeric to Hellenistic times and from Athens to Alexandria, one can say that it was above all concerned with inculcating a style of life, and like the education of a young man at a mediaeval or Renaissance court this was seen as part of, not as additional to, a liberal education. It is true that mankind has an immense debt to those outstanding Greek thinkers who carried the concept of reasoning far beyond any previous point in our history, but this should not be confused with the general picture.[16] In the same way our schools are the only social institutions, in effect, for promoting the continuous and systematic cognitive development of the young and it could be argued that this gives them their distinctive importance. But this would seem to many people an overstatement still. An equally important role, not only in schools but in a liberal education, is the introduction of the child to a whole range of experiences, often with a cognitive element but basically imaginative and expressive rather than cognitive, which help him to realise his potentiality for valuable and sensitive living. Professor Hirst gives this a kind of admission but he consistently underplays it.

He says of 'artistic judgement or emotion' (phrases that are really not adequate) that it is the concepts they employ that determine their character. He does not elucidate this or give examples, and the phrase seems to me an unhappy one. In the study of literature and the arts there may be technical concepts involved, but these, though interesting and sometimes necessary for full understanding, are not the most important thing. Otherwise there are no concepts that are different from those of our experience in life. And concept is not really the key word. A poem is a statement in the sense that the poet is saying something, of course; but not in the sense that the propositional and conceptual features of it are the poetry. The interest and the value of the poem lie in the range, intensity and imaginative excellence of the communicated experience that is the poem. Unless this is really grasped as the essential thing in literature and all the arts of expression, one half of the curriculum for a liberal education will be planned on the basis of a wrong idea and we shall have, not a liberal education as Matthew Arnold understood it, but an illiberal one as understood by James Mill, whether 'utilitarian' or, as with Professor Hirst, exclusively dependent on some other kind of philosophy that is educationally too cognitive. It is because I feel this very deeply that I am impelled to disagree with Professor Hirst.*

* I had written this chapter before reading Professor Elliott's criticism of Professor Hirst, the latter's reply, and the former's counter-reply in the symposium edited by S. C. Brown, *Philosophers Discuss Education* (Macmillan, 1975). This controversy has a curiously double air of forcefulness and thinness. Elliott's main charge is that Hirst's account of Understanding does not allow for its psychological basis: the public Forms of Knowledge are made logically prior to the natural powers of the mind. There is indeed, Elliott says, a common or natural Understanding irrespective of learning that takes place through the academic disciplines. On this point I think Elliott is right though I agree with Hirst that he makes too sharp a difference between these. One merges into the other. I think the commonsense view would be that from

Having seen, then, in three important examples how theories trying to be comprehensive, but starting from only partial truths, end by being misleading, let us take our courage in our hands and look at the problem of getting the most appropriate curricula in our schools from a more commonsense point of view, despite the warnings against the pragmatic that we are so often given.

Some of the current confusion undoubtedly comes from not sticking to the plain meaning of the word curriculum. With many writers it has become unduly inflated. Cynics may amuse themselves with the thought that the word comes from the course, laid out in advance, for a strenuous and highly competitive chariot race: an apt analogy, they will say, with our secondary education. The idea, applied to schools, is simply a course of studies laid out in advance. But some of the contemporary pundits go much further than this.

Professor Kerr[17] starts modestly enough by defining the curriculum as 'all the learning which is planned and guided by the school', but then he widens this. He says there are four elements in the curriculum: objectives, knowledge, learning experiences and evaluation. Now it would seem to me that your objectives in doing something are not part of that something, and your evaluation of what you have done is not part of it either, any more than the announcement that you have just had a good dinner is part of what you have eaten. This is confusing.

It does not follow that because two things have a close relationship they are part of the same thing. It is true enough that the curriculum almost always needs to be considered in relation to the methods by which it is taught. Professor Bruner says, 'a curriculum is a thing in balance that cannot be developed first for content, then for teaching method, then for visual aids, then for some other particular feature'.[18] But to use the word curriculum for all these things collectively deprives us of useful and necessary distinctions. How else can we say, for instance, that the curriculum of a school emphasises the classics but that methods of teaching the classics are

---

the exploratory movements of a baby onwards we do have drives that make us want to understand and that our success or otherwise depends largely on our general powers of mind; but that in an educated man these are shaped, improved and occasionally distorted by the disciplines he follows. It seems rather obvious. However, because Elliott sees the importance of this psychological basis he can continue, logically . . . 'It is difficult to regard a psychical power used in two different disciplines as two entirely different powers when introspective analysis reveals an identity or close similarity of structure. When we think of understanding in terms of psychical powers it seems that it is the same Understanding which is active in each domain, and that the logical differences spring from differences in the nature of objects towards which the one Understanding is turned, or from differences in what we are interested in in the same objects.' (This is very much the point I made on page 21.) In his counter-reply Elliott says that if the criteria of truth are distinctive, indeed unique, in each Form of Knowledge, there can be no standpoint outside a discipline from which they can be criticised. The disciplines do not determine what Understanding is, but exist to help better understanding. But if, as sometimes happens, they do not, there must be criteria external to each discipline to entitle us to say so. I think Elliott is right in this, and in general I find his criticisms convincing.

very old-fashioned, or that the curriculum consists of the traditional arts and sciences but neglects the social sciences? It is confusing to make the word curriculum virtually identical with school education in all its aspects.

We are also losing a useful distinction at the opposite end of the scale. Curriculum used to stand for the total programme of studies. When we wished to speak of the course of study in a single subject we used the word syllabus. In England, ever since the Schools Council came into being, curriculum has been used for the part as well as the whole. At first sight the Schools Council and the Nuffield Foundation have been very active in curriculum reform. In fact almost all their work has been in particular subjects or subject areas. We have had little consideration of the curriculum as a whole. There has been some debate as to whether the secondary school curriculum should be as specialised as it is, and a few writers like Professor Lawton have given attention to the whole; but when you ask what serious examination and what reform there has been as to the total curriculum you have to reply, practically none. Our misuse of the word has disguised this.

How do schools come to have the curriculum they have? I would say, slightly adapting a phrase of Professor Lawton's, that curricula consist of those studies and experiences selected from the culture of communities as the most important to transmit to the next generation and as suitable for doing so through schools. But some of the terms in this statement need definition themselves.

The word 'transmit' may make this description of a curriculum look conservative. It is true of course that schools are among the institutions through which one generation passes on to the next the knowledge and the style of life that it thinks important. But it is also true that the tradition of our type of society includes among its most cherished values a belief in the critical intelligence; so that part of the tradition we pass on is not to be content with tradition. We do want the schools to play their part in giving each new generation not only the knowledge and the skills they will need but the understanding of our way of life that, as we see it, will help to make life worth the living, but we do not see this as at all incompatible with the fostering of individual judgement and taste and distinctive personalities.

Although in practice there may still be much to do, there is not much need now in circles where educational theory is discussed to stress the need to think of children and young people in their own right and to stress their development rather than externally imposed requirements. This has been a good influence, by and large, in the last few decades. But the 'philosophy' behind it has sometimes been naïve. I think especially of the notion that all we have to do is to allow children to develop 'naturally', and that the role of the teacher is simply to put them into what are called 'learning situations'. I think, on the contrary, that both teachers and parents have a positive, not just a negative, role to play. I felt that it was a kind of sentimentality of the Plowden Committee to call its report *Children and Their Schools*. It is good to hear children say with a touch of pleasure and pride, 'That is our school', but in sober fact the schools are not the children's; they are the community's. When it comes to deciding what should be taught the professional voice should be listened to with great respect (else why have a teaching profession?) as well as that of the lay community, and each of these should have the interests of the children in the forefront of their minds. There must be a conversation in which all these three voices play their part and exclusive claims by any one of them must be resisted. This, it would seem to me, is the commonsense of the matter – not easy platitude (for it is often forgotten) but the commonsense that should always be in mind. At the present moment in educational discussion it is probably the interest of the community that is most likely to be overlooked, and Professor Lawton is right to bring attention back to it.

The word culture also raises questions. One can take it in the way anthropologists do and think of the curriculum of a school as a selection of what is most important in a whole way of life, its knowledge, its use of artifacts, its style of living. But the word selection turns the meaning towards high culture, the narrower sense of the word, the finest flowering of the human spirit in the arts, science and civic and individual life. Yet this is too restrictive. In a general system of education schools should open the world of culture in this sense to all who will enter, and should encourage them to do so. A school with an anti-cultural or anti-intellectual ethos is a bad school. Yet, as Professor Hirst says when speaking of a liberal education, there will be, inevitably and rightly, other things too: practical activities and pre-vocational skills, physical education and games, and studies that while properly to be considered educational are not at this conscious level of high culture.

The uncertainty about the word culture in fact reflects a tension that one will expect to find in any school. The sensible middle position may well sound a little equivocal, but it is defensible. It seems to me that a secondary school as well as a primary school should above all give a good general education, but as distinct from a primary school should not in its higher forms have a common curriculum. After having satisfied this need for a good general education a school should beware of making certain studies prestige studies, in the sense that Latin was once considered indispensable for a man who would be taken to be educated and sketching and ability to play the piano absolutely essential for a young lady who wished to be considered accomplished. In spite of being on the whole a francophile I think there is a 'tyranny of French' in our curricula today and that there ought to be a wider effective choice of languages in our secondary schools. I think that philosophy, although many of my French friends say how much they have owed to the system, has held too high a prestige place in the French *lycée* (it is beginning to change now). Culture, even high culture, is nearly always a wider thing that our schools have wanted to recognise, leaving out of account the difficulties of wide provision in the smaller schools.

Yet I would not agree for a moment that Shakespeare, let alone Dickens, are 'middle-class' interests and for an elite only. This notion, oddly, comes from some members of the would-be left as much as from the right. Not merely should the door be open to all; all should feel they have as much right to enter as anyone else. Not all will want to come in; but they should be shown the way if they wish to take it. When I think of the Leeds bus-driver who wrote for me as good an essay on the Brontës or of the plumber who wrote as good a paper on Kipling and the sons of Martha as any I have had from university students, while I know that they were exceptions, I grow very impatient with this myopic view of culture in relation to social class.

On the other hand again, there is a kind of 'soft' egalitarianism that does betray standards in the name of human sympathy. I do not believe that the Beatles (or whoever is top of the pops now) are as good as Beethoven, and however tolerant a school may like to be to current popular music (and let us concede that there may indeed be musical skills involved) it should not give the impression that they are.

It may look at first sight as if it would be difficult to make a synthesis from these 'on the one hand, but on the other hand' statements. In fact I not only think it is possible but would defend it as the only kind of synthesis that makes sense.

The third word in this description of the curriculum that needs some elucidation is 'community'. Really it should be in the plural, not in the singular, for we all belong to more than one community. There is of course the national community to which we belong; but increasingly as we think of preparing the present generation for the future we must give a world dimension to our studies and understand that for many important purposes we now belong to an international community, however imperfectly served as yet by firmly established institutions. Then, at the other end of the scale, there is a school's local community. And finally many private schools serve a special community, often though not always a religious community. By and large it is legitimate that all these communities should make demands upon their schools that relate to what is taught in them; and there may be a need for adjudication between apparently conflicting claims, the most difficult being to decide how far, if at all, there should be support from the general community for separatist religious schools which, as in Northern Ireland, may contribute to the sectarian divisions that make a genuine national community so difficult to attain.

Let us now switch the point of attack and look at the curriculum in terms of what we teach in successive stages of a school education.

There is now not much disagreement as to what should be done in the early years, say from 5 to 9 or 10. Children should be introduced, without rigid timetabling and with relative informality, to the main areas of what will later be a more structured curriculum. They should get a reasonable command of the English language, first in speech and then in reading and in writing. They should have the first ideas and skills in what will later be mathematics. They should have an introduction, both descriptive and exploratory, to the world of science and get the first idea of what it is to experiment. They should get to know about the social world around them, including what will later be fully fledged geography and history. And they should be encouraged to express and develop their experiences through the arts, especially music, drama and painting. To this I would only add that there should be plenty of healthy and pleasant physical activity and that moral education, even though not called by that name, should be taking place all the time.

Although there would be little disagreement about this there are one or two points of controversy over the curriculum even at this stage. If the environment of the school involves the use of more than one language there is a good case for the study of a second language at the higher end of this age-range, but in general I see little need for it yet. Again there has been criticism of 'progressive' education because it is said, with or without foundation, to let the children play happily without teaching them to read and use numbers effectively. I would only say that these skills are basic and must on no account be neglected. But two points are to be remembered. First, panic sometimes starts too early with parents: children learn to read at different ages and there is no necessary cause for alarm if it comes a little later rather than a little earlier along this time-scale. Secondly, taking reading seriously in a school does not mean simply clinging to old-fashioned methods. Teachers are conservative enough not to need a reinforcement of conservatism from parents who want their children to be taught very much in the way they were taught in the schools of a generation ago.

One other matter of controversy should be mentioned though I shall discuss it more fully in a later chapter; that is religious education. In societies like our own we recognise the right of groups of individuals and of communities within society to found their own schools if they wish to do so. Most of these schools have been established by religious communities that wish through them to pass on their own religious views and attitudes to the next generation. This right should be respected; but on the other hand the community as a whole has a right to ensure, through inspection, that such religious education is not conducted in a narrow and intolerant way such that acceptance of fellow citizens of different views as good men and good fellow citizens is made more difficult. In the publicly owned and maintained schools the case is different. In these, in our multi-belief society, no particular religion or view of religion should be given official preference. Indoctrination of the young (for this is what it comes to if there is an officially approved religion for schools) and the performance of religious ceremonies to which probably the majority of the parents pay no heed themselves should be left to the homes and the churches and not be part of a school curriculum.

What should be the general nature of the curriculum over the next stage of school education, from the age of 9 or 10 to the age of 15? The important change from the previous period is not so much one of content as of attitude and method. I should describe it as a transition from learning through play to learning through work. Now spontaneous interest is not enough. The idea of steady application has somehow to be instilled without dulling natural curiosity or imposing a merely dull routine on the young. This raises very difficult questions as to methods of teaching in this age-range. I am sure that it is not enough to do what the Plowden Report essentially recommended, to project the methods of a lengthened infant school upwards into the primary school; and certainly not into the lower secondary school.

There are two major questions to decide in our mind about the curriculum at this age, as distinct from teaching methods. One is, how far it should still be one for general education, virtually common for all, and unlike the division that Professor Bantock, for instance, recommends between the book-minded and the rest. The second is, how far subjects should be taught separately and how far studies should be integrated. This second controversy continues into the higher secondary school but it first raises its head in arguments about the curriculum in the age-range we are now considering.

As our national societies have developed during the last hundred years they have continuously needed better general education for the ordinary citizen. In the public systems of education the miserable fare of the old elementary school has given way to the idea of a broader education up to the age of 15 or 16. In the independent and fee-paying secondary schools the curriculum has also widened from the classics and little else to a general curriculum of arts and sciences up to the fifth or the sixth form. The need for a longer and more general education has been recognised, whether for the generality of young people or for those who will enter the professions. But in England specialisation starts sooner than in Scotland or the Continental countries or the United States. What developments are we likely to need in the future?

The speed of social and technical change produces the need for a longer general education, not the opposite, as has sometimes been supposed. In the economy the proportion of people needed for the unskilled and semi-skilled jobs is falling. Those with the background for skilled work and the increasing number of recognised professions are increasing, and the higher the technical or professional level of work the longer the general education required. In skilled, though not fully professional jobs, it is more important to grasp general principles and to be able to learn new processes than to have been drilled in processes that in any case will soon be out of date.

The argument from the quality of our social life is no less strong. For our societies to have good standards, in literature and the arts, in civic conduct and public morals, there must be a shared consciousness as to what is good. Minority insistence on good standards is very important, but, as I have said, a healthy minority culture today is not viable in a general cultural morass.

All this points to the need for a sound general curriculum at least up to the end of the secondary school. It need not be absolutely identical for all. Some, but not all, will want to have started a second foreign or classical language before the end of this period. Some measure of emphasis for those who have gifts in a special direction (in music or mathematics, for instance) would not be unreasonable. But the broad aim and the broad achievement should be a common general education up to the age of 15 or 16.

But, it may be said, is not this just what we do now? Not altogether, I think. I freely concede that some progress has been made. In the public schools the move towards the comprehensive principle has at least given a framework within which the idea of a common general education has more chance than it had in the culturally impoverished secondary modern school and the separate academic grammar school – but only the framework. A great deal depends on what actually happens inside the framework; and at present there is the greatest variety, in practices and in general level, among schools all labelled 'comprehensive'. I am not saying, as some reformers do, that anyone can learn anything, given enough time and help, that the only difference between individuals is in speed of learning. This is just not true. But it is nearer the truth than some teachers assume. That is why in the controversy over 'streaming' the middle course seems to me to make most sense. General streaming, the separation of pupils into groups each of which is fixed and covers all learning, seems to me deplorable at this stage. This way we label boys and girls as A types, or B, C or D types for all purposes, almost in their whole personalities; and this seems to me thoroughly bad. On the other hand there is a good deal to be said for 'setting', that is to say for a measure of separate teaching for those who are especially good at one thing or slow at another. This is most clear in a study like mathematics, but also notably in music and art and in languages. I think there is something in the argument that to have to wait for the slowcoaches is frustratingly boring for some one who is bright; and that you pile up difficulties for the slow or ungifted in some particular study if you have always to be pressing him to keep up with the rest.

I see no harm, and considerable advantage, in such modifications as these in the principle I have enunciated. It seems to me that the principle, of a general education for all up to the age of 15, is not yet as firmly established as it should be, and that the level of staffing and equipment necessary to give the flexibility that is called for has not yet been achieved.

It has been in the grammar schools and the independent schools that the idea of a really general education has been most transgressed, the compensating elements being that there has often been a considerable activity of a general educational kind through extra-curricular school societies and that many of the youngsters in these schools have come from educated homes. But in some of these school specialisation has started at a ridiculously early age, not simply at 16 but at 15 and even 14. There has been protest, and some organised opinion forming, against this; and there has been some improvement. I know of one famous independent school, taking boys at the age of 13, that was virtually three separate schools, in terms of curriculum, from the start; and I am told that happily the picture is considerably different now. But I don't think that anyone, looking at what is done in the best secondary schools in other countries, can feel content. We still tend to specialise far too early.

But this is only the beginning of my criticism. A more important point will come out if we ask the question, when should differentiation in the curriculum begin in a decisive way?

When we raised the school-leaving age in England what we did was to keep in school a large number of young adults who wanted to be out in the world. In the secondary school we do little to tell them about the world of work, wages and young adult social life into which they are going. And this is something that they are very much interested in and concerned about by the time they reach the age of 15. I would ask for a decision (taken firmly, but not irrevocably) as to whether they intend to leave school at 16 or stay on till 18. For those who propose to leave I would devote the final year to three kinds of study: one-third would be continuing studies of the normal kind, with scope for choice; one-third to pre-vocational education in an area of their choice; and one-third to an introduction to the adult social world.

I would relate the third kind of study closely, though certainly not exclusively, to the immediate locality, for this is where these young adults, at any rate at first, will mostly work and live. There has been increasing awareness in our schools of the educational potential of the immediate environment. Arnold Bennett now would rarely be able to make the complaint that he did about young Edwin Clayhanger, who, although he was taught geography at school, did not know why there was a canal under the bridge he was leaning on in his Potteries town, had no idea why there were barges on it, and did not know what they brought into the Potteries or took away from it – in short, did not know how his own town made a living. But if we tell the young now a little more about the geography, the history and the ecology of their locality we exploit very little the opportunity to introduce them through the locality to the structure, the norms and the problems of human society. A minority of schools do plan some community service or bring local officials and even professional people and workers into the school; but there is still great unused scope here.

For those who plan to stay on at school I would subsume this kind of experience into sixth-form studies and I would fuse it with more academic teaching. Highly theoretical teaching of sociology and economics is still not altogether appropriate and such studies would be largely descriptive, but the serious discussion of leading concepts (class, race, social mobility, industrial relations, unemployment, inflation) is certainly possible. There should of course be plenty of opportunity, as with the lower age-group that leaves school at 16, for the treatment of controversial topics in discussion rather than teaching sessions. But for the sixth formers there should be structured courses, not just 'topics'. The aim should be to give those who are going to end their formal education at 16, and those who are going on to higher education but are fully ready by now for educated awareness of the social world around them, the introduction to adult life they need and that society needs them to have. But from the different circumstances of the two groups the teaching style must be different enough to warrant a branching of the curriculum at the age of 15. For the first group I do not have in mind simply an O level in sociology, but something much broader. For the second group a broadly conceived A level might serve.

But with this kind of curriculum what happens about the school-leaving examinations? I would say, let us for once practise what we preach and make the examinations follow the curriculum. In my opinion there should be at most one school-leaving examination for any youngster, and it should come when he is about to leave school. It should be on the actual course of study he has followed, and this, on the plan I am suggesting, would be somewhat different in the two cases. Every one should have a school-leaving certificate and there should be a limited number of grades, perhaps three in all, for each paper or practical examination taken or each assessment given.

There would have to be flexibility for two classes of student. Some at present stay for one more year after 16, but not two. This I would strongly discourage. Either 16 or two more years should be the norm. For those who announce that they are going all the same to leave after one year in the sixth form there should again be a school-leaving certificate based on the course they have actually followed. Then there would be the students who have changed their minds. If they had said they would leave at 16 but changed to 18 then they should not take the examination at 16 but the one at 18. If on the other hand they had opted for 18 but find, perhaps because of changed family circumstances, that they must leave at 16, then once again they should have their leaving certificate after an examination in what they had actually done. Even with these two escape clauses the plan I am proposing would be essentially simple and cut right through the jungle we have made for the young ever since the perversion of the original proposal for a single examination in which papers could be taken at two levels made in 1949.

The two simple principles behind this scheme are: (i) that every youngster leaving school should have a school-leaving certificate, and (ii) that this should attest what he has done at school and not aim also at deciding on university or other higher education entrance. For this latter purpose the levels gained in the school-leaving certificate should be taken into account to the extent, and no more, that past performance may be held to afford evidence of likely success in a future course in higher education. The institutions of higher education, in the three main groups (and not acting individually) should set their own prognostic tests, whether by formal examination or aptitude tests or a combination of the two; and their right to select their own students should be safeguarded by not conferring a right to entry as a result of success in either these or the school-leaving certificate but leaving each institution, in accordance with interviews and the number of places it has available, to admit or not to admit after taking all this evidence into account.

If studies designed to give knowledge of the adult social world are one of the real gaps in our school curricula today there is another that is no less serious: that is moral education. It might, of course, be considered that moral education comes under the general heading of introduction to the adult social world, but I think it warrants special consideration for itself. It astonishes me that there should be any hesitation about this, as if it were not quite proper in a school curriculum. All educational history shows how important human societies have known this to be. And we do very little about it.

One explanation of this is that moral education was long supposed to be part of religious education, about which I say more in Chapter 4. Religions have of course had their related moral values and religious sanctions have been invoked against immoral conduct. Yet, in terms of principle, theology and ethics are not identical studies. And in terms of practice now in multi-belief schools such an association, apart from the impossibility of making it acceptable to all parents, has broken down. However closely individuals may relate their religious and their moral outlooks, moral education should be recognised as something to which we should pay attention in its own right.

It is also said that a sound moral attitude is something that is better caught than taught. There is much truth in this – but not quite enough. It is probably the best principle to go on in the early years, but after that stage we surely leave out something of great importance if we do not accustom young people to ask the question, what ought I to do, and why? Once again, this question should be put and discussed in terms of particular problems, but especially in the sixth form such study can be structured so as progressively to bring out the meaning of such terms as rights and duties, the individual and society, custom and morality, and so on. In the sixth form it could, without being pretentious, be a first course in ethics.

It is in the lower secondary school especially (though to some extent in the upper secondary school also) that the question arises as to how far the curriculum should consist of separate subjects and how far subjects should be integrated for teaching purposes. There has been theorising about this, but it seems to me that the question is above all a practical one: how can what is to be learned or studied be learned or studied with the greatest educational benefit?

The most recent theory about this has put forward the thesis that this is not just a question of teaching method, but of social controls. The argument is that the very way knowledge is transmitted is related to social structure and particularly to the retention of control by the socially dominant groups. You may indeed look at both primitive and modern societies and find some evidence of this. The tribal bush school of pre-technical West Africa, in which the young were initiated into the ways of the tribe, was firmly in the control of the elders and certainly buttressed their position. It could be argued that in post-Napoleonic France the structuring of the transmission of knowledge through the *lycée* and the *grandes écoles* has kept the key positions in the hands of an elite, with a career open to the talents of only a few newcomers (if they adopt the life-style of the class they enter). But to be fair one would have to put against the *Polytechnique* the *Ecole Normale Supèrieure*, with its long record of critics of French society from Jaurès and Léon Blum to Jean-Paul Sartre. I think some of the proponents of this idea go much too far, making truth and knowledge far too exclusively relative to the class structure at a given time and overstating the link between curricular style and social attitude. The argument seems to be that willingness to break down subject boundaries always goes with openness about social reform or revolution, and respect for subject divisions with a general determination to maintain class barriers in society. I am only partly persuaded. It may be only that persons who are by temperament or interest conservative in one thing tend to be so in others. That the most important consideration is practical – how something can be learned and taught best – is clear if one takes examples. The argument against 'integrating', say, French and Indonesian, is not ideological. It is simply that if you try to teach them both in the same period, although they are in the same area of learning, that of languages, you will not learn much of either.

The sensible answer will be different at different stages in education. In the early years, although specific times may be set aside for some specific things, there should be great flexibility. Young children should be encouraged to follow where their curiosity leads and not shut off an interest because they are not doing that subject now. What used to be called 'Nature Study' is much better at this stage than formally divided botany and zoology. When you are out walking nature does not confront you for three-quarters of an hour only with flowers and in the next only with animals. It seems to me that general science has a great deal to commend it up to the age of 15 or thereabouts. I am less persuaded of the case for integrating history, geography and civics in the lower secondary school. Perhaps we are overinfluenced by the not very happy American experience in doing this. I think the basic difference between general science and general arts is that there is more of a general scientific method applicable to what later may become separated subjects of study than there is a general arts method applicable in common to history, geography, civics and (as is sometimes claimed) English. In the sixth form I am sure that the case for the study of separate subjects becomes extremely strong. This is obvious earlier in studies, like mathematics, that are sequential; but it seems to be strong in other areas too. I doubt if you would get far in music if you studied music only as it was incidental to dance or drama or whatever it was integrated with.

The remedy for exclusiveness when there is not formal integration is surely that teachers should be ready to combine with their colleagues wherever this can be profitable, rather than remaining shut up in their subject. I recall one school which had for a term a project on the eighteenth century as the age of taste in which the history master and the craft master collaborated to great effect. There should be much more of this. The virtue of it, as distinct from overintegration, is that the teacher is not called upon to range so widely that his professional conscience is, or ought to be, uneasy. A teacher of intellectual integrity will hesitate to teach something in which he is not really competent.

In Australia I met a chemistry teacher who told me she had been pressed to teach physics in her school. She could manage first-year physics not too badly, but no more; and she was uncomfortable about it. I think it is very important to respect such a scruple. I might also have said (though I did not) that perhaps her training had been rather narrow, and if it had been she might still have supplemented it later. Still, I do respect the scruple. I am afraid that just because memorable writing is about such a vast range of things teachers of English are especially tempted to go outside what they really know (to make rash historical generalisations, for instance, or give rather uninformed views of social processes) and in such cases 'integration', as distinct from collaboration with well-informed colleagues, can be intellectually shoddy.

Were I a headmaster I would not be dogmatic about either integration or collaboration. So much depends on the actual people you have on your staff, and they must each of them lead from strength. Some are wider in their interests and competence than others. I would encourage more experiment, especially in team teaching.

What is sometimes forgotten is that this debate is not the same one as the debate about general as distinct from specialist education. You can certainly get a very good general education although you study a considerable number of subjects separately. The French *lycée* and the German *Gymnasium* show that. I am certain that our upper secondary education is too narrow. Mr Peterson showed in his Gulbenkian study *Arts and Science Sides in the Sixth Form*[19] that the average sixth former would like to study (even for examination) more than the three A level subjects that he now substantially does, and that his French and German opposite numbers would prefer fewer than the nine or ten they commonly carry forward to the *baccalauréat* or the *Abitur*. I am sure their instinct is right.

There has been talk of overspecialisation in our universities. The two or three subject degree is becoming rather more popular (I still think, however, that the Cambridge plan is the soundest: an honours degree in two parts, which can be either in the same subject or in two different ones, but in the latter case with the two subjects taken in sequence, not at the same time). But I would not be worried very much by specialisation at the university if our secondary schools made it quite clear that their function was to give a *general* education. More specialised education and training, for industry, the professions or academic life as it may be, should come after that. This is the basic principle on which our secondary school curriculum should be built: not a uniform and compulsorily common education, but one that begins like that and then increasingly allows of choice, so long as the result is a general education, not premature specialisation.

Many more particular matters of course remain to be discussed: the degree to which a world dimension must now increasingly come into school studies, and related to that our policy in regard to the study of modern languages; the need to be discriminating in the use of that too popular word, 'relevant'. (It is absurd that throughout the Commonwealth schoolchildren know more about the defunct British Empire than they do about the living Commonwealth of today. On the other hand contemporaneity is not a sufficient guide. I once heard Sir Richard Livingstone say that it is more important to know about Socrates than about Napoleon.) Here I must be content with the main points I have tried to make.

These, as will have been seen, I have made in the light of two guiding ideas, the needs of society and the needs of the young, but essentially my stance has been pragmatic. And this, as I noted earlier, is frowned on by some theorists of the curriculum. But I have looked at three particular and influential theories and none of them seems satisfactory. In such a situation, so long as our proposals have been seriously thought about and are founded on good arguments and good sense, need we be ashamed of being pragmatic?[20]

Chapter 2

A Particular Case: The Classics and the Ancient World

I noted in the last chapter that what is taught in schools does change as societies change. This causes painful problems of readjustment. Those who have followed and perhaps taught the old studies have to choose whether to refuse to recognise the facts and to go down protesting, or to face them with good sense, make their accommodation and save what they feel to be most valuable in the studies they love. Nothing illustrates this better at the present time than the dilemma about the classics.

In our civilisation the classical languages are Greek and Latin. But every civilisation conscious of its origins is faced with the same kind of problem that confronts us. When I was in India as one of the foreign members of the Government's Education Commission I heard anxious discussion as to the place of Sanskrit in their studies. Again, I have heard it said that if we want to see what it means to cut off a civilisation from its classical past we may soon have a laboratory example in China. The attraction to the authorities of modernising the Chinese language (a task not so easy in practice) may lie not only in the efficiency to be gained but in the increased difficulty of access that would mean to old ways of thought that the regime does not favour.

Another point worth noting is that although Greek and Latin are our classical languages, in the seventeenth century Hebrew nearly made the grade and was indeed taught in some schools. Translations of brilliance may more than make up for the falling away of wider studies of the language, so long as some scholars remain. Since Hebrew has ceased to be taught to non-Jewish boys and girls, Old Testament scholarship has advanced, and until the last generation or so knowledge of the Old Testament has been spread much more widely through translation. Those who insist overmuch that ancient Mediterranean civilisation cannot be studied without its dominant languages might reflect on this. For us the term 'classics', thought of in relation to schools, means primarily the languages of Greece and Rome. It implies some knowledge of Greek and Roman civilisation, but that claim only becomes real at the level of the university. Faced with the paradox that the fruit of all this hard language labour was hardly ever reached by the average schoolboy subjected to it, must we not ask whether more understanding of the ancient world might have been gained by the much wider use of translation?

It was this fruitless grind more than anything else that produced such anger and frustration, especially about the turn of the century when in so many of the schools that counted then it was the classics or nothing. Kingsley Martin told the familiar story in the first volume of his autobiography.[1] He says that he spent nine years at school studying hardly anything but Greek and Latin, and he says about his visit to Greece later: 'When I saw the hills around Athens crowned with violet I could not quote Sophocles in Greek. As I came through the Vale of Tempe and saw the great block of snow which is Mount Olympus I did not care a cuss that the words that came into my head were mainly English. I say this to encourage some other Mr Polly who discovers Greece but does not know Greek.' In fact Kingsley Martin was far from being a Mr Polly and he had in formal terms a chance Mr Polly never had. Somehow his interests should have been aroused at school and when he came to Greece those nine years should not have seemed wasted. (I might add that I myself never had this traumatic experience. At my municipal secondary school I had a good Latin master, though I wish I could have done more of it, to get to the point of real use for enjoyment. And I would indeed have liked to have Greek, but my school did not teach it.)

One thing is absolutely certain. The study of Greek and Latin is never again going to occupy practically the whole of a school's timetable as until recently, in the great independent schools and many grammar schools, it did. This monopoly position was almost certainly an educational *dis*-advantage, for it led to the dreary conservatism of teaching of which Kingsley Martin complained. Now that there cannot be such a near-monopoly we are forced to come back to what Milton said over three centuries ago.[2] He said two things about the teaching of Latin and Greek. He poured scorn on the teaching that makes a boy 'spend seven or eight years merely in scraping together so much miserable Latin and Greek, as might be learned easily and delightfully in one year' – a view that has been ascribed to his supposing that all boys were as apt to learn as John Milton, but in which we might admit that there is something, now we can teach languages like Russian and Japanese in much shorter time than used to be needed. Secondly, Milton asked why we learned languages, and insisted that they were to be regarded as means, not as ends in themselves. He says: 'We are chiefly taught the languages of those people who have at any time been most industrious after wisdom; so that language is but the instrument conveying to us things useful to be known.'

If we do devise better methods for teaching Latin and Greek, and make them much more relevant to the civilisations of which they were the tongues, can we expect now to find a reasonable number of boys and girls, with all the competition from other subjects, who want to take them up? 'Fit audience let me find, though few', if I may echo Milton again, may be a phrase by which a teacher of classics makes a virtue out of necessity. But if the audience are too few that consolation will hardly be enough. Is Greek, and even Latin, to go the way Hebrew went? To answer this question we must ask why some young people want, actually want, to learn Greek and Latin, and how this number might be increased.

Most people who would hate to see the classics go down are not so much worried about the languages themselves. What is to be feared is that this decline might lead to a sadly diminished knowledge and understanding of the ancient world. This is the serious danger. Only through some better combination of the languages and the study of the civilisations can we meet it with a rational hope. As Dr Bolgar said in the first number of *Didaskalos*:[3] 'The future of classical learning depends on our being able to show that it makes a valid contribution to man's understanding of his world and therefore to the betterment of life. We must therefore, in considering the possibilities of the subject, take our stand on the fund of human experience which it reveals to us.' This is essentially the position that Milton took.

If understanding of the ancient world and its civilisations is the most important thing, we have to consider whether command of its two main languages is indispensable, and for what level of understanding; and if it is in general desirable, but as a means rather than an indispensable thing that becomes virtually an end in itself, we have to ask whether it might be second in the time sequence of study too. We have to ask this question if we believe that knowledge of the ancient world should be available for everybody in our world of general education, and this means a major readjustment for people brought up in the classical tradition. The classically educated minority of the past was an elite, but in this elite community everybody did make the classics very nearly the be-all and end-all of education. Within this limited community, beginning with the languages and going hard at them for year after year worked reasonably well. There was no serious competition from other studies and no problem of mass education. This worked for the cultivated minority at any rate until the later years of the nineteenth century. It gave us leaders of our political and cultural life who, when they were not confusing us with the Chosen People of the Hebraic tradition singled out for special favour by God, were confusing us with the citizens of Rome who had a worldwide mission of peace and law. We may laugh a little; but these were noble illusions, and not entirely illusions either. This minority of influential educated men felt the culture of Greece and Rome to be their culture. This sense went beyond the ranks of the influential on the national scene. If we think of Charles James Fox and Macaulay and Gladstone, we also remember the perpetual curate of Hogglestock.

For reasons that are familiar enough this will not work now in our society. There isn't the necessary support in our cultural milieu for starting the young on Greek and Latin at a very early age, making these their main studies for ten years or more and following through at the university in the hope that a genuine sense of the ancient civilisations will emerge. At most this will be the choice and the reward of a very few. Now we have to look at the opposite possibility, that a desire to master Greek and Latin may emerge because a good number of young people have discovered an interest in the world in which these languages were once spoken. Some may in fact have started at least Latin and find they wish to go on to Greek; others may be later starters in the languages because they find they want them to satisfy their wider interest. The new emphasis will be on the ancient world and what it can yield for our own lives and the languages will be seen as the means to understanding it for those who wish to take this to any serious depth.

What are the arguments we can bring forward for the view that an understanding of the Graeco-Roman world is important, not only in terms of a limited number of genuine scholars who can increase that understanding, but as a desirable part of any good general education?

First, it is specially and peculiarly our own heritage, as of all European peoples. There is no need to expand this statement; it is so familiarly true. But I would like to make one or two comments. First, in some respects the claims have been exaggerated and this has done the cause no good. It is not true that a knowledge of Greek and Latin is indispensible for the writing of good English. Bunyan and Cobbett alone disprove that. But a feeling for that ancient world is highly desirable, and very nearly indispensable, if one is to write with any fullness of human experience about our civilisation itself. Shakespeare may have had little Latin and less Greek but the ancient world was real to him (even though without the kind of historical accuracy we now demand). It was part of the very stuff of his experience. So was Greece to Keats. Again, it is not indispensable for a lawyer to know Latin. The Latin tags that have been said to serve too often as a substitute for principles in English law may be picked up by anyone, whether he has Latin or not. But to understand the role of law in civilisation would seem to me impossible without some sense of law in relation to the world order of Rome; and in fact that English law owes little to Roman law is likely to be less of a cause of insular pride now that we have rejoined Europe. Again, the generalisation that the Greeks of the fifth and fourth centuries BC, especially in Athens, were clear-minded critical thinkers, needs many footnotes. There was a primitive, even at times a superstitious element in common Greek attitudes to life, as well as a non-rational ecstatic one, to which increasing attention has been given in recent years. Yet it is still true that we could hardly have learned to think, or have formed the very categories of discourse, without the great thinkers of early Greece. And our civic sense is still rooted in the experiences of the Greek city-state and of the Roman city that became a great republic and an empire.

These things are important, not just for a few specialists, but for everyone. A man in our cultural tradition who has nothing of this furniture in his mind has simply not had a sufficient general education. You cannot understand the present without a sense of the past. This is our past, or a most important part of it, and I would say a more important part now than the Hebraic tradition. It may or may not be more important than the Christian heritage, but that itself offers a remarkable and subtle fusion between the Hebraic and the Graeco-Roman.

I would also like to make a specifically educational point about the study of the ancient world of Greece and Rome. The beginning of wisdom is in the making of critical comparisons. To know what is good and what is bad, what is beautiful and what is not, what is true and what is false, you must compare things: statements, buildings and other works of art, persons, actions and ways of living. What has been the classic comparison between ways of life from the time of Pericles and Plato to our own day? The comparison between Athens and Sparta. It is a theme that can still get schoolboys talking. In one form or another this is a perennial theme in human history, and although one may find analogues in many cultures this particular well-documented comparison is distinctively our own.

For the full educational effect of such comparisons the less familiar culture must be near enough to their own for the young to feel inside it with the right effort of learning and imagination. Yet the two must be unlike enough for the comparison to be instructive and to help form genuine powers of discrimination. This, whether you are discussing philosophy, art and literature, or politics and general history, is exactly what the ancient world of Greece and Rome offers us. It is like enough for problems in human conduct to be fairly posed. To make this point by contrast: think of the difficulty of understanding nepotism in some non-European societies where not to use your office to assist members of your family is simply to betray a loyalty. I have always been rather horrified by that story of the first Brutus who put the State so far above his natural affections that he did not hesitate to order the execution of his own son – with rather better cause than Abraham ever had. But no one brought up on that story could doubt that there were situations in which wider loyalties must over-ride even loyalty to one's own family. What is open to discussion is how far this can reasonably go. One can discuss the conduct of Brutus and discriminate between the stern mores of ancient Rome and our own society, which would condemn interested attempts to thwart justice but would not expect a father personally to judge and condemn his son.

Or take the second Brutus we have all heard about. Here was a man who had been treated almost like a son by Caesar, whose most serious love affair had been with Brutus's mother. It could be that personal vanity weighed most with Caesar in leading him to assume a regal and quasi-divine state; but the effect of doing so on the prospects of Rome in Egypt and Parthia may have weighed with him more. Yet Brutus, who was an honourable man, joined in the conspiracy to kill Caesar because on principle he thought dictatorship wrong. Then, if one story is true, he was so disturbed in his inward mind because of this, that his stroke missed and he only cut himself, an omen of his own death to come. There are similar dilemmas in all history, with differences that are as instructive as the similarities.

Was the dilemma of Falkland insoluble in the English Civil War? Was Mirabeau right or wrong to open correspondence with the Royalists after the first phase of the French Revolution? What of the agonised night when in the end Lee decided to break his oath to the United States and side with Virginia in the American Civil War? All these cases, different as they are, teach one thing, and this is the great thing that history does teach: that in a crisis we have to make up our minds how to act on a balance of judgement, not from certainty that any facts can give. The evidence is never so unequivocal, the argument never so conclusive, as it is for the scientist in his laboratory; and the decision in our minds can never be as clear-cut. In the world of ancient Greece and Rome we can study such problems of human conduct in a setting near enough to ours to make them real and yet different enough to distance the discussion and free us from the immediate pressures and prejudices of our own time. In our civilisation this has been part of the best education from the Renaissance reading of Plutarch till yesterday. It should and could continue, though there may be few who read about these matters in the original Latin or Greek.

I said, could continue. But can it? There are still some who say that it must be virtually a closed book if we do not have Latin and Greek. Perhaps here I may speak of a personal experience. In 1945 I became Principal of Ruskin College, the college for workers' education in Oxford. Here were our students, men and women mostly in their later twenties, back from the armed forces or war industry and determined to get the mental equipment to set the world to rights. I can still remember their looks of astonishment when in my first lecture on political theory (which I was taking till we could get a specialist on the staff) I said we should study only one book in our first term, and that an ancient one, Plato's *Republic* in Cornford's translation.[4]

We had no Greek and did not mistake ourselves for scholars in Plato. But we could compare one translation with another, a point that went home through Cornford's remark that Jowett's rendering that to be virtuous we should study philosophy and music did not mean that to save ourselves from irregular relations with women we should practise on the violin in the intervals of studying metaphysics. We learned something about Greek concepts from the notes on them given by translators, and particularly Ernest Barker in his translation of Aristotle's *Politics*. We asked a classic or two in the university to come and lecture to us and bring Zimmern up to date; and of course Sir Richard Livingstone came to talk about the significance of these things for contemporary adult education.

Then a party of German educationists came to visit the college. They could not believe that such study could be serious without a knowledge of Greek. While they were right at one level, this view was too narrow. I invited them to visit our students in their rooms, to see if the *Republic* was on their shelves and to discuss it with them. At the end of the week they told me that obviously something was working here and having an effect on minds. I hope we avoided the danger of too slick comparisons. But we did discuss questions that were perennial, yet always different because of the different forms they took. When we discussed Plato's view that a statesman should have true knowledge and not merely powers of persuasion the relevance to our own politics (and, as one student said, to the way some trade union leaders attain to power) was not to be missed, though the kind of knowledge Plato required was not precisely the kind of knowledge we might recommend for a statesman today. Some of my students of those days are now indeed in positions of authority and I would like to believe that they do not look back on that term as wasted time. What I am sure of is that what they could do (most of them at that time without any secondary education) many more, youngsters and adults, could also do.

If this is what we are going to attempt there is one great, and in a way unexpected factor on our side. The growth of interest in the ancient world has been astonishing. People, including schoolboys and schoolgirls, go to Greece and Italy now and something stirs in them when they do. Even the professional classic, who gained his impression of Greece from those sepia photographs (with a stain in the bottom corner) or some ruin or other with the sunlight left out, in the past often never got to Greece at all. Now the sunlight on the broken column can be every man's experience.

Another important sign is the remarkable increase in the number of translations from Greek and Roman literature. Thirty years ago there were very few translations into good contemporary English: Cornford's *Republic* and Barker's *Politics* and of course the plain text Loeb Classics. There had been no sustained effort to give the English reader the great Greek plays since Gilbert Murray made his translations into the poetic idiom of the end of the nineteenth century. The English reader who had been told how good these plays were had to make a remarkable effort of charitable imagination when he tried them in the stilted versions then available. Classical scholars (with honourable exceptions like Gilbert Murray, Lowes Dickinson and Alfred Zimmern) did not think of themselves as serving the English people, but just the few who had good Latin and Greek. If the Greek plays were acted this was almost always on a picture-frame stage, and when one adds the language into which they were rendered the effect was ludicrous. I saw one performance of the *Antigone* where a human thought had to struggle through lines like 'O happy 'tis when he who deems deems just'. I remember thinking that if that is the influence of the classics on English style, heaven help us!

Now things have indeed changed. The Penguins deserve our great gratitude. From the day Mr Rieu's translation of the *Odyssey* appeared (and it has sold, I believe, some 5 million copies) we have had translation after translation into good, vigorous and sensitive English. There is a public, young and old, that wants to know about Greece and Rome and to read what was written there. And it wants to see what was built. The third factor to note is indeed the great increase in public interest in archaeology since Sir Mortimer Wheeler made his first appearances on television, for classical archaeology came into this. These diggers and decipherers from Schliemann to Ventris really have become part of 'what every schoolboy knows'. People do not merely listen when scholars say these things are significant. They are excited by them themselves.

All this should give a great opportunity to classical studies. But it depends on one thing: making knowledge of the classical world the first thing, in importance and to a considerable extent in time sequence, and not doing things in the traditional way, the other way round. This does not mean that the teachers of the languages need be fewer, or less important. One advantage of the fairly large comprehensive school is that it can have a larger staff, with more specialists (there are comprehensive schools now that teach not only Latin but Greek as well). But I am making the claim that if not all then a large majority of our secondary school students should get some knowledge of the ancient world, and this means that the classics teacher must be willing to come outside his own classroom, to collaborate more. I know one school where the headmaster, formerly a teacher of biology, was asked by a team of teachers giving a sixth-form course in the history of ideas to contribute three lectures on Greek science. He told me he had not had to work so hard for years, and he had thoroughly enjoyed the experience. More of this cross-fertilisation is needed.

Some of those who doubt such departures, if more than occasional, say, how do you fit all this into the timetable? Well, timetables were made for man, and not man for timetables. Certainly, if you give time for the study of something such a group of students has not studied before, you do have to take time from something else. But if the case has been made out, why not? If we broaden the sixth-form course and the main diet of three A levels gives way to five or six subjects, those will not be A but A-minus levels. The question is, not the timetable, but the course to be adopted on educational grounds.

The structure of the secondary school sequence alarms some teachers of the classics more than timetabling as such. We have considerable variety in this country in the ages of transfer from one school to another. If boys and girls do not come into the secondary school proper till the age of 13, it is said, how can they be prepared in time for their Latin or Greek O levels? There will be short-term difficulties until we do reform our public examinations system, I would hope in the sort of way I suggested earlier. But it is still true that the commonest age of transfer to the secondary school is between 11 and 12, which gives time enough even on the old assumptions about examinations. The general answer is commonsense flexibility. I have, for instance, never understood the intense reluctance of most teachers to teach in more than one school, if they are reasonably near to one another. In federal universities university teachers often lecture in more than one college and certainly take students from more than one. If a locality has a system with middle schools there is surely no reason why, if some of their boys or girls want to start Latin or Greek in the middle school but not enough to warrant full-time staff members for that purpose, teachers from the senior secondary schools should not take them.

The real change we need is of a different kind. There will always be a few boys and girls who want to start Latin early and follow it a year or two later with Greek. This will not absolve the teachers of those languages from working out ways of teaching the languages more effectively and in a shorter time than in the past. The key to this, as contributors to *Didaskalos* have said and as the new Cambridge Latin Course has shown, is to concentrate on what we want Latin and Greek for: to read, not to write. If there is practice in writing that should be for the purpose of reading more exactly, not as an antiquarian end in itself, as it has been (verse and all).

For most, however, an introduction to the ancient world will in the future precede the study of the languages. This introduction should come very early in the secondary school (or in the second half of the middle school if that is the structure of the system). It could certainly be made interesting to the generality at that age, and without sloppy popularisation, which no one wants. After one or perhaps two years of this there should be a new 'set' for those who had been stirred by this experience to want to start Latin or Greek, or both. In any secondary school now there is a large proportion of youngsters who round about the age of 14 feel themselves strongly drawn to the humanities, but few of them feel that in addition they are in a position to become specialised 'classics'. Some of them are made to feel, in the present system, that even if they would like this it is now too late. Others, three or four years later, may wish they had gone farther along this route. It is very important to give the boys and girls who find they do want the classical languages a second and even a third chance; to have more than one point of entry to the classical languages. The third chance should come when they have entered the sixth form or the sixth-form college. We really cannot believe that with modern methods of language teaching a two or three years' course of Latin or Greek, taken with the intensity that is right for language study, and with the stronger motivation that these students will have, is pedagogically unsound. At this age you learn more quickly than you do when a child, and if you make the decision yourself you want to go fast.

Many details would need to be worked out, but I have a strong feeling that such a recasting of classical studies would now make very good sense. We have much more potential interest than before, and knowledge of the world of ancient Greece and Rome is still a desirable part of everyone's education. What we have to do is to recast our teaching methods and our structures now that everyone means everyone and not just a few in a limited number of schools. Essentially this means three things: making economies in the time needed and by concentrating on the reading, not the writing, of these languages; allowing more than one point of entry to their study; and above all restoring the proper order of things by treating the languages not as ends in themselves but as the means to a fuller understanding of the roots of our civilisation. An increasing number of teachers accept this and try to do it now. It certainly seems to me the commonsense of the matter.

Chapter 3

Liberal Education Reconsidered[1]

If, as we have seen, the place of the classics in our education needs to be thought out afresh, what shall we say about the concept of a liberal education, which the classics fathered?

It was a concept that originated in a Greek society very different from ours. It had a new lease of life in the nineteenth century, from whose social structure we are moving steadily away, while some countries have thrown it over altogether. Is the idea so imbued with these circumstances first of its birth and then of its revival that it would be only misleading to make it an ideal now? Or are these social characteristics of its previous formulations only accidents, leaving us a vital idea that we could well take up with renewed devotion and reinterpret in terms of our own times?

Certainly it is a concept that refuses to die easily. It is one that nearly every philosopher of education of our own day has at one time or another examined seriously and usually with sympathy. Those who are impatient with it feel that the phrase has become a device in the hands of traditionalists pleading for the retention of education for gentlemen that should be swept into the dustbin of history now. I am as strongly against class distinctions in education as anyone, but the phrase and the concept are ones that I find I cannot give up. The idea, despite its social accretions from the past, stands for something valuable, at least as I see it, and something that it is difficult to express in any other way. Whether, not analysing the concept with the detailed rigour of a philosopher but applying a more general educational good sense, we can reinterpret it usefully in present-day terms is what I would like to discuss in this chapter.

Let us look again, even though it be familiar matter, at what the ancient Greeks, and especially Aristotle (since he stated his views at some length) understood by liberal education. Aristotle's views are to be found chiefly in his *Politics*, itself an interesting point; for it would occur to very few of our writers on politics to include in their works a detailed indication of what should be taught at each age to the children of their state, and yet education is indubitably political. In his discussion Aristotle continually says what he thinks is an appropriate education for a free man. This of course is the root meaning of the phrase, a liberal education.

But what is a free man? For Aristotle and his contemporaries, in the first place, a man who had that legal status, who was not a slave. But we have to get behind this easy distinction. What mattered was the kind of life that was open to each. The free man was not overburdened with material cares, the slave was. The free man had his duties, but he could be himself as the slave could not. The slave was someone else's living tool. The free man could rise above the tyranny of immediate circumstance; the slave hardly could. This is the important distinction to keep in mind. There were, to Aristotle, pursuits that were liberal and pursuits that were illiberal, but the kind of life that a study contributed to was more important than, as we would say, any distinction between subjects.

It is not difficult to see that the young must be taught those useful arts that are indispensably necessary; but it is clear that they should not be taught all the useful arts, those pursuits that are liberal being kept distinct from those that are illiberal, and that they must participate in such among the useful arts as will not render the person who participates in them vulgar. A task and also an art or a science must be deemed vulgar if it renders the body or soul or mind of free men useless for the employments and actions of virtue. Hence we entitle vulgar all such arts as deteriorate the condition of the body, and also the industries that earn wages; for they make the mind preoccupied and degraded. And even with the liberal sciences, although it is not illiberal to take part in some of them up to a point, to devote oneself to them too assiduously and carefully is liable to have the injurious results specified. Also it makes much difference what object one has in view in a pursuit or study; if one follows it for the sake of oneself or one's friends, or on moral grounds, it is not illiberal, but the man who follows the same pursuit because of other people would often appear to be acting in a menial and servile manner.[2]

Here indeed it all is, the enlightened man and what we, unhistorically, might be tempted to call the snob, apparently inextricably mixed! Can they not be disentangled?

If we leave on one side the argument that becoming highly skilled like a professional makes a man too one-sided, and if one accepts the fact that in Aristotle's Greece brutally hard work had to be done and that slaves did it, what is Aristotle really saying? He is saying that the mind and the personality cannot flower as they should if a man's work is degrading and he has always to be preoccupied with material cares; that one cannot live a good life if one thinks only of what is useful, not of what is enjoyable and good to do for its own sake; that always to be at others' command and to have to do things because they say so is incompatible with being free.

Now the legal distinction between the free man who need not work and the slave who does nothing else has gone. But is not Aristotle's essential meaning, as I have rephrased it (I think fairly) very pertinent still? To be free enough of gross material cares to experience more of what life really has to offer; to be in command of our own faculties and not to have to use them merely for our own or other people's necessities, but for living a life that is good, so far as the human situation allows: this is to be free. A liberal education is one that helps to form the mind and indeed the personality so that this becomes possible.

Before looking at the curious transmutation of Aristotle made by our immediate forebears let us ask what sort of things we have in mind by such a liberal education. If it is to be an education befitting a free man, and the legal distinction between a free man and a slave has gone, what is a man so educated to be free from?

In the first place, from ignorance. A man cannot have had a liberal education if he is not educated at all. But we mean more than that, in terms of knowledge, when we add the word 'liberal'. We imply a width, a range of knowledge. The narrow specialist, however remarkable, is not someone we should describe as having had a liberal education. We mean something, however, that goes even beyond this. The liberally educated man will not know everything, but he will be free of the kingdom of knowledge, in the sense that he has a wide range of interests but also has learned how to learn, to turn them into genuine acquirements of his mind. What this range at a minimum should be is a matter for debate. We associate the term 'a liberal education' with the humanities rather than the sciences, and on the whole I think rightly. But hardly any one now would consider a man or woman liberally educated who had no curiosity about the sciences, knew practically nothing of any of them, and did not understand the kind of contribution they make to a life that is to be liberated from ignorance.

Secondly (and very much connected with this first point) we imply that a man of liberal mind is not a pedant, not a dogmatist by invariable nature, not sectarian and not given to at least the grosser superstitions. These are all difficult terms, but collectively they do indicate what we should not consider liberal. The notion 'free' goes naturally with the notion 'open'. The unfree man is bound by his prejudices. The man of liberal education feels free to consider (even though in the end he firmly reject it) any proposition for which evidence is brought forward and that can be rationally defended. His liberal education has led him to be open to reason and his knowledge and training have equipped him to test assertions openly and fairly.

Thirdly, there is a generosity about men of liberal education. They are free from meanness about ideas and motives. They have a largeness of mind and spirit. They are free equally from the vindictive and the servile. They have dignity; but they do not always stand upon it.

Most important – and here we are very close to Aristotle – the man of liberal education has the power to rise above immediate circumstances, and above all above immediate material circumstances. He is free from the merely material.

This may sound like a catalogue of all the virtues. But it is not. There have been many men who have earned respect, and some very remarkable men, who have not had these liberal virtues. There are other virtues: courage, moral rectitude, determination, simple integrity, and a kind of wisdom, maybe narrow but deep, learned from a good upbringing and a felt experience. But persons with these qualities are not, without something more, men and women we should describe as of liberal education. The qualities I have mentioned do make up much of what we should hope for in a completely admirable human being, but they are not all that go to that. Although my terms have been wide, they are discriminating, between the liberally educated man and the man who is not. I think, also, that they are what Aristotle had in mind, the social context having been, so to speak, transcended.

Now in the nineteenth century in England there was a taking over, and at the same time an interesting transmutation, of the idea of a liberal education as expounded by Aristotle. (I am not unaware of the educational influence of Aristotle in the intervening two and a half millennia or so, but from my present point of view it is what happened in the period immediately preceding our own that is of most significance.) The big difference between the Victorians and ourselves in the framework of educational discussion is that for them, until towards the end of the century, this was chiefly that of the 'Public Schools' – or, as I shall call them, the independent schools – whereas it is now primarily that of the public education system.

For Aristotle's 'free man', since everyone in England was legally free, the Victorians substituted a related but not identical concept, that of the 'gentleman'. The gentleman, educated in the independent schools and often Oxford and Cambridge, was like Aristotle's free man in that he was expected consciously to rise above the vulgar, and of course the menial and the servile. There were no slaves, but there were the masses of industrial workers (wage-slaves as they sometimes described themselves, with some anger) and almost endless lines of servants. There was also a very well-marked hierarchy in society, with some mobility (much more than in Aristotle's Athens) but mobility that it usually took more than one generation to effect, either upwards or downwards. The status of gentleman, as that of the Aristotelian free man, indicated an ability to live without engaging in manual labour. These were the social and economic bases. There was also a strong feeling that being a gentleman implied something in style of life and manners; and indeed something about virtue in character. All these things were reinforced by the education the gentleman received.

I suppose that if you are not a peer, have no occupation and can live on money you do not earn, you inscribe yourself as a gentleman. But the idea that even if you can live on your unearned income this exempts you from work has almost disappeared. There can be few boys at the independent schools now for whom the question of a future career is not a serious one. This change was shaping itself during the later part of the nineteenth century. Aristotle conceived of the leisure of the free man as being in part for worthy enjoyment, but chiefly for pursuing virtue, personal and civic. This made the Victorian transmutation easy. A transmutation there had to be, for otherwise the ideal would have come into conflict with the tremendously serious Victorian gospel of work. It was made through the idea of the liberal professions. These were the professions that a gentleman could, and increasingly should, enter.

A liberal profession was not one without its financial rewards. Indeed these were commonly high in relation to the standard of living of the average man. But they were not usually as high as those of successful industry or trade (the risks were less too) and in a liberal profession gain was not the over-riding motive. This was very evident in the Church, medicine and teaching, and it was to some extent present in the law, since a successful barrister who became a judge made a financial sacrifice in doing so. Just as the idea of the free man who did not need to work was turned into the idea of the gentleman for whom the primary purpose was not financial reward, so the idea of study that was not to be entered on for reasons of usefulness was turned into the idea of knowledge that could be studied because it was also of interest for its own sake. Thus both hard work and financial reward were liberalised, at least for the socially dominant sections of the community.

This was the most important shift in the Aristotelianism of the education of the gentleman up to the time of the First World War. To make a more thorough study of it one would have to pay attention to all sorts of components in the total social and educational picture, some close to, some farther from, the original Aristotelian conception of the right education for the leisured free man. There was the ideal of public service, civilian or military, for instance, which was very much in accord with the Greek ideal (as distinct from Victorian individualism, which was not). It was, perhaps more professionalised. Yet this professionalism, to risk a paradox, was oddly amateurish. The officer in the army, outside the more mathematical branches, had little training that was seriously professional; the chief things were to have courage and to be a gentleman. The schoolmaster was expected to know his matter, but he had no professional training of the kind we think necessary now. The Church of England clergyman was expected to be an educated man, but again being a gentleman was the chief consideration, even more than being serious about religion until the nineteenth century had run a good part of its course, by when it came indeed to be stressed. The civil servant of the second half of the century was still very much an amateur, and proud of it. The duties were not exacting: Trollope, employed in the Post Office (and by his own account rather more industrious than the average), could still ride regularly to hounds and write a prodigious number of novels. There was even a minority cult towards the end of the century of the idea that the more useless knowledge was the more excellent and honourable it was. This was outside the Victorian main stream, but it was especially fashionable in late nineteenth-century Oxford.[3] Allied to this was the style of 'effortless superiority', again encouraged in late nineteenth-century Oxford. It was in part a pose (Jowett was an incredibly hard worker) and in part could be justified as an outward and visible sign that however busy a gentleman might be he would not make a parade of it and always had time for the minor, but so valuable, courtesies. Allied to this again was the notion that the educated man had had an intellectual experience that was infinitely transferable, professional knowledge and experience in a relevant context being of little account, the professional expert indeed being only too likely to have a warped judgement. This notion has now been abandoned everywhere except in the British civil service, where to know how to administer is to know how to administer anything. Proficiency in Greek verse used to be considered quite a good indication that you could administer a colony, and if it has ceased to be so that may be because we do not now have any colonies to administer.

These things were encouraged, one might even say inculcated, in the influential schools of the day. The inspiration came from a remarkable (and indeed at times very odd) fusion of the Greek ideal of the free elite and the Christian gentleman. The idea of Jesus and his disciples as gentlemen would be historically very odd, so odd that it was not made a direct ascription; but the concept of the Christian gentleman nevertheless runs right through nineteenth-century upper-class education. (The reaction of a few priests with a radically different social outlook, like the late Conrad Noel, was to portray Jesus as a proletarian revolutionary, a kind of leader of a non-existent Communist Party of the day; and this is equally unconvincing.) Charles Kingsley, introducing *The Heroes* to the children for whom these Greek stories were retold, said they were not all true of course 'but the meaning of them is true, and true for ever, and that is – "Do right, and God will help you" '.[4] A more grotesque confusion (and a less historical one, from a professor of history) between the morals of the Greek pantheon and that of Christianity it would be difficult to imagine.

Yet the fusion worked and was real in the minds of Arnold's Rugby boys and their successors there and in other independent schools. So did the fusion between the Aristotelian ideal of the liberally educated man and the gentleman who conformed to the Victorian gospel of hard but not mercenary work. Here, however, one must note an influence that is sometimes forgotten. When people say Greek they commonly mean Athenian. The Victorian independent schoolmaster meant something else: he meant Spartan. In the popular sense these schools were indeed Spartan. As one former Eton master once said to me, 'The function of the Public Schools is to make the British ruling class tough'. As a classics don and clergyman, originally from Charterhouse, also said, 'At such schools you learned that you had to have guts'. After our experience of totalitarian regimes we tend to see the Athens–Sparta polarisation through Athenian eyes. In the independent schools of the nineteenth century things were not so one-sided. Indeed one is almost shocked now to find the admiration of Spartan ways in such a book as *Schools of Hellas* written by Kenneth Freeman, the brilliant young classic of Edwardian England.[5] So were the liberal and the illiberal intertwined.

Apart from this there were two things about these schools that characterised their transformation of the ideal of a liberal education. The first was that their curriculum itself was almost entirely based on the classics. The study of Latin had been part of a vocational and professional education; it was not only useful, it was essential, up to at any rate the end of the eighteenth century. (Greek, with the Renaissance, added something that was more clearly humane and less directly useful.) Then the usefulness of the classics gradually became less obvious. There were still two lines of defence. One was that they were still useful through the inculcation of mental habits that could be transferred both to other studies and to real life; and the other, related, argument was that the classics formed the mind to discriminate justly, to have a fine sense of private and public duty, and to form the tastes that befitted a gentleman in literature and the arts. Sometimes these arguments were carried to absurd lengths. Leslie Stephen, writing the life of his brother,[6] recalled their time at Eton:

> Balston, our tutor, was a good scholar after the fashion of the day and famous for Latin verses; but he was essentially a commonplace don. 'Stephen major', he once said to my brother, 'if you do no take more pains, how can you ever expect to write good longs and shorts? If you do not write good longs and shorts, how can you ever be a man of taste? If you are not a man of taste, how can you ever hope to be of use in the world?'

In the finest examples these transferences could be seen to have worked well, but most young men, as we have seen, hardly ever got to this point, and classical scholarship hardly bore out the point unequivocally. There has been a tendency, evident even in the humanism of the Renaissance, for classical scholarship to run to grammar and pedantry. I remember how surprised I was when I came up to Cambridge to read the summaries of the meetings of the classical research society: it seemed to be all about conjectural emendation of texts and nothing about what the texts as wholes said. A. E. Housman, I was told, gave a whole course of lectures on Catullus without mentioning that he was a poet. Scholarship's proper concern was with the text. It was this kind of perversion that drove Professor Trevor Roper (he says) from the classics to history. History at least could be about the important things. The classics should have been. A. Gilbert Murray at Oxford, and a small group at Cambridge, did see classical scholarship in a wider context, but it is difficult not to conclude that predominantly it had become illiberal. Aristotle had paradoxically been proved right at his own expense and in his own domain: it is not so much what you study but why and how you study it that matters for a liberal education. That is a point, as we shall see, that is important for answering the question as to what constitutes a liberal education now.

The second thing that made the independent schools up to 1914 so influential in forming the notion of what a liberal education was has more to do with style of life and with subjects studied. Our independent schools, like those of Hellas, were at least as concerned with inculcating a style of life as they were with formal cognitive achievements. Their significant contribution was in making the amateur gentleman ideal influential. This was felt in general, but it was achieved especially through the ideal of the gentleman amateur in sports and games.

There was ample Greek warrant for serious attention to games and athletics as part of education, but Aristotle drew a clear distinction between the training of an athlete and these activities as part of the education of the ordinary free citizen. He said: 'The athlete's habit of body is not serviceable for bodily fitness as required by a citizen, nor for health and parentage. . . . The bodily habit therefore should have been trained by exercise, but not by exercises that are violent, and not for one form of labour only, as is the athlete's habit of body, but for the pursuits of free men.'[7] The (as we might say) professional athlete was overtrained in some one direction and this put his life out of balance. This view is not far from our notion of the difference between the amateur and the professional. But once the practice of organised competitive sport for grown men comes in there is a complication: the amateur is not merely the keen all-rounder who plays for fun, he is the man who is wealthy enough to be able to do so without payment, and a very real class distinction is thereby introduced.

In the early days of the Rugby-type schools in England, according to Mr David Newsome,[8] the motto was 'godliness and good learning', but this gradually changed to 'godliness and games'. In more recent years things have come better into proportion. If you want to feel the full force of the total commitment to games now you find it in some of the independent schools of Australia and New Zealand. But in general society in those countries the stratification, or comparative lack of it, is different from that in England, so that the passion for games is not associated with the class distinctions that have accompanied it here.

It is difficult to see how the amateur ideal could have survived once the economic basis for it had gone. We have had the rather hypocritical transition period of the 'shamateur', and in the revived Olympic Games there was for many years a great effort to save what was said to be the Olympic ideal (with doubtful warrant from antiquity, according to Professor Moses Findlay). The communist countries don't believe in gentlemen anyway and have had no compunction about making their athletes officers in the army or giving them other kinds of lucrative recognition. In this country in cricket the distinction between amateurs and professionals has pretty well broken down (how eloquent was the old term, gentlemen and players!) and in that at least we are catching up with the Australians. The distinctions between the more and less gentlemanly sports are going (Stanley Matthews the footballer in the end got his knighthood like Jack Hobbs the cricketer, though he was first fobbed off with an OBE). Professionals in games, especially in football, are earning much larger sums, and this is tending to increase rather than lower their social standing. These changes have not affected schools directly, but they have affected them indirectly, in giving a different image of what should be admired. Some see this as a gain, because it has eliminated a good deal of snobbery; others see it as a loss, because it has produced increased admiration for the professional who makes his living from sport and less for the man who plays games for fun. What is certain is that there has been a modification of the notion of a style of life that was once very much part of the education, in the wider sense of the word, encouraged by the privileged independent schools. It did permeate general society. The working man spectator often gave an extra cheer for the spirited amateur, the Corinthian, even if he lacked the expertness of the professional. He would not do so often now.

Perhaps this is the moment to draw up a balance sheet, to decide for ourselves what was good in the idea of a liberal education, touched as it was by class bias, and to see whether we are in need of such a conception any longer. And since we have been discussing the amateur ideal that was very much one of its components we might start with that.

There are two questions to be asked: how far does being a specialist and a professional really distort the personality, and how far does doing something for pay corrupt?

It is not a question of scorning the greater skill and knowledge of the professional. Even Aristotle never said that there should be no professionals or specialised athletes. Some amateurs of course have admired the skills of the professionals. Probably most of them have. But it has been admiration *de haut en bas*. Many, including Aristotle, have disdained them. I don't think anyone in our society does. And are we really convinced that their lives are all that distorted, except in a minority of cases? The professional footballer or cricketer is not distorted physically by his profession; he is rather developed thereby. Nor is there any reason why his abilities in general or his personality should be so distorted, unless he cannot withstand the temptations of commercialism (and that is our second point). Aristotle is as down on the professional musician as the professional athlete. Would we say that following music as a profession really distorted the personality? It does lead a person to become one-sided in the sense that he devotes himself to one thing, but it is through that one thing, music, that above all he realises his personality. Nor is there anything to prevent him from being generally well-educated and interested in many things, like Mr Yehudi Menuhin for instance. Surely, to become a gifted professional musician is not to condemn oneself to being an illiberal person. In this we must reject Aristotle entirely.

The professional, it is true, has a commitment that the amateur does not have. He is committed to playing, whether musically or athletically, even if he is not in the mood at the moment. The amateur can please himself. That is to say he can consult his immediate enjoyment more. But any good professional feels that this very commitment, though it may go against the momentary grain, deepens his satisfaction. It is the pride of the actor, who really is not well, but prides himself on taking the stage because 'the show must go on' and he is 'a good trouper'. There is a profound satisfaction in being really competent in something. This satisfaction the professional can enjoy; the amateur can 'have fun', but that is a different thing.

It is in a minority of sports and other occupations that professional dedication can distort. The weight-lifter or shot-putter who is already grossly overweight but feels he simply must put on another couple of stone (and knows that his rival may be taking steroids to do it anyway) is the man who will distort himself physically. It is his decision. If he will sacrifice even his chances of surviving healthily into old age for the glory of competitive success, then all right. He chooses so – and good men have chosen so before him. But he is not an example for the ordinary man, and still less for the ordinary boy. At the other end the jockey whose weight has been contrivedly kept down when young may win the Derby, but a wrong, a distortion, has been inflicted upon him. These are indeed a minority of cases. This is not true of the average professional in either the arts or sports.

The one touch of truth in Aristotle's criticism seems to apply particularly with young adults, often but not only at the universities. It is true that standards of performance in athletics have gone up and it isn't possible any more to get your 'blue' or the equivalent just by a certain natural ability and an hour's casual training fitted in between lectures. You have, as the Americans says, to 'go out' for track or whatever it may be. I rather applaud the man who still runs or plays but won't be 'dedicated.' He will probably miss his 'blue', but have much more chance of a liberal education. I prefer the attitude at Harvard, where they try as hard as anyone in the eight or on the field but don't feel that the world has ended if they lose, even if they lose to Yale.

But what about payment for unusual skill? Payment as such, indeed high payment, is not the evil. Why should not a fine musician command a good fee? And why not a star professional footballer, at least while occupations that give less harmless pleasure are so well rewarded? The danger is not payment as such, but a certain kind of commercial exploitation and the resultant pressure to win at all costs. 'Nice guys come last' is a nasty phrase. To lament professionalism is to luxuriate in pointless nostalgia. It is more important to make sure that these are good professions – to keep out the bribers and corrupters and check the players and spectators who lower standards – than to cry for an amateurism that has gone. The effect of the standards of the professionals is very great, for they are still the schoolboy's heroes. If the word 'gentleman' has an outmoded sound, produces the wrong image somehow, what it stood for in behaviour is not out of date. This needs restating in contemporary terms. The wrong pressures from outside make the honest sportsmaster lament. But there always were such forces, from the time of Arnold's Rugby till now, and a good school has always had to struggle to be better than its moral environment. If one believes that education is concerned not only with the cognitive but with style of life – with character, if the old word does not grate too much – then this is important. The embarrassing thing about so many of the Speech Day cliches is that they are often at least half true. What is learned in games does carry over into life. If sometimes we feel that this country needs to reassert the will to win it needs no less to revive respect for the courage to lose. To learn magnanimity is part of a liberal education as well as to learn to love literature.

There would, I think, be little disagreement with the statement that this, and the other qualities I associated with the idea of a liberal education, were desirable in themselves and should be in our minds very much in the education of the young. The question rather is whether bringing them together under one concept, that of a liberal education, is still useful now that education is concerned not only with an elite but with the total mass of our young. It seems to me that it is, because this gives a focus, a conscious aim, to what we ought to be doing. But the reasonableness of that assertion depends in turn on how effective such a focusing in the new conditions can hope to be.

The first thing to note is that we are speaking of an aim. Making all education truly liberal never succeeded even with the privileged groups of Greece or the English nineteenth century. The majority of these never became truly liberal men. Matthew Arnold and Newman who alike raised their voices in terms of the qualities in education that I have described here as liberal would have been astonished at the suggestion that even the most influential groups in society were liberally educated as a whole. To be realistic, then, we must put the question in a different way: how far does it make sense in our mass society to hold to liberal education as a conscious aim, at the very least to aim at liberalising it more than we do at present? In answering this question, what are the factors we have to consider?

The first problem – and here we come oddly back to Aristotle – is the nature of so much of the work that has to be done. Though ours is an industrial society and his was not, we are up against the same problem. Can a man whose daily work is 'alienating' (to use the current term) be a man of liberal mind and education merely in his leisure? If he is such, how could he possibly tolerate such work? This is a question that goes beyond educational policy and this is not the place for a thorough treatment of it; but something must be said, for it is a question we cannot avoid.

Our image of the worker in modern industry is of the man on the production belt. He works to the machine, not the machine to him. The pace is set for him. His operations are for the most part routine. The noise is deafening, the air dirty, for all the Factory Acts. His human self is hardly called on at all. How far is this image really right?

It is broadly right of a considerable proportion of modern machine industry, and because it is typical of what is most recent in human history we take it as typical in the sense of being general. There can be no doubt that it 'alienates'. Half the troubles in labour relations are obviously the result of these general conditions: 'reasons' can always be found for this or that sudden stoppage, but they are not the underlying reasons. If the conditions of work make men bloody-minded what else can you expect them to be when they negotiate with the management? And how can you expect them to spend their leisure in what a liberally educated man would consider a civilised way?

In principle there are two ways of dealing with this problem. Higher wages, though they may help to reconcile people to this sort of work, are not really the answer. One answer is to mechanise still more, so that hardly any human labour at all is needed. There certainly is some scope here. Years ago it was said that if it were desired even a car could be assembled without the touch of a human hand. But that means that men lose their jobs and the resistance to labour-saving devices, though irrational from the point of view of the country as a whole, raises endless difficulties of gradual phasing out of now superfluous workers. One may doubt if this will ever give the complete answer.

The second policy would involve a deliberate decision to forgo some of the advantages of assembly line production to make work more worth while for those engaged in it. This does not mean always forgoing the machine. Who would want the old drudgeries of the farm to come back, or sweated household industry? But it does mean a limited withdrawal of the apparent primacy of production in favour of other values. It does not necessarily mean less actual production. At least one Swedish car firm is forming teams of workers to be jointly responsible for producing a car engine in the hope that their group interest will get rid of the bloody-mindedness induced by the belt that makes such fertile soil for rows and hold-ups of production.

A great deal depends on the length of the working day. Ten hours a day of such work is one thing. A four-hour day, reasonably well paid, would be quite another. Even now no one would have the impertinence to suggest that workers in the car and similar industries are brutalised in the sense that slaves were in the past, or even coal miners and peasants and some other workers in earlier Europe. Liberal education is going more and more to be a matter of adult education, not only of schools; and it seems to me that if we value such progress and are willing to make money available for it we have cause for some anxieties, but not for pessimism.

What is not true, however, is that this is a typical image of the worker in industrial society in the sense of being almost universal. Far from it. Years ago Stuart Chase showed in his *Men and Machines*[9] that if modern machine industry had invented the assembly line and its routine work it had also brought into being a great number of new callings that did involve personal involvement and responsibility. The car does come off the assembly line; but to keep it on the roads there have to be great numbers of garage hands whose work is varied, skilled and responsible. The plane is a product of modern technology; but the maintenance staff and the air crew and the airport staff are not robots. The lorry driver is no robot either. The proportion of workers at the point of production gets less with every mechanical advance, the numbers in distribution and white collar jobs more. To draw up the balance sheet is not easy. On the one hand the old crafts have mostly gone, and the new craftsman of the machine does not shape things himself in quite the way that the old leather worker or smith did. But on the whole there is surely less drudgery now in industrial England than there was a hundred years ago. It is less the relative actual state of things than, rightly, the consciousness of rising expectations that is producing the protest and the call for a revision of the values of industrial society. If either socialism or capitalism is to have a human face, a reorganisation of our industrial life, with genuine involvement of workers in what they do, has got to take place. Without this it is vain to expect the ideal of liberal education to be widespread. It has been remarkable over the last sixty years or so that the Workers' Education Association has stood firmly for liberal, as distinct from merely vocational, education, and with such a genuine degree of success. It is so far from being a criticism of it that its members are now studying economics less and the humanities more: this is really a vindication of its whole liberal education stand. Our provision for adult education of all kinds does not compare badly with that of other countries, but with a humanising of industry it could sweep forward with greatly increased support.

Within the schools the first problem we have to face is the extent and nature of general education, for a liberal education, though not the same thing in idea as a general education, depends upon it as its basis. I have put the case for regarding the whole of secondary education as general in the first chapter of this book and here I shall supplement this only with one or two comments.

The universalisation of secondary education since the last war has left us still without a clear and good enough idea of what and how we should teach the majority who would not have been in the academic secondary schools before this change. For this previous smaller secondary school population, specialisation came too early, but it was not too difficult to say what we meant by a general education up to the end of the lower secondary school. Furthermore this minority mostly came from homes where there was a fair level of general education. The new majority mostly came from homes where the parents themselves had had only elementary schooling. What was clear was that a simple extension throughout the post-war secondary schools of the general education of the academic secondary school, with its traditional methods as well as its limited subject matter, would not do. This was what those who instituted the tripartite division of secondary education saw, but their division was not the right answer and it only dodged the problem. Some of the secondary modern schools and some of the comprehensive schools showed initiative, but by and large this problem is with us still.

It is to be seen much more dramatically in France, where the *lycée* was more severely intellectual than our grammar school, where the famous *culture générale* for which it stood was more of a professional class thing than our equivalent, and where the teachers even till now have had hardly any training preparing them to deal with this, to them, alarming new intake. According to *The Times* supplement on France of 25 November 1975, the secondary school intake in France increased from 692,000 in 1945 to 3,923,000 in 1974, five and a half times as many. According to the same report the pupils are openly indifferent to the old values and complain that they are forced to swallow a dead culture that does not interest them. This is a very serious situation indeed and it is interesting that the Minister of Education (M. Haby) proposes to deal with it first by establishing a single-type comprehensive school that will give a solid general education to all, including elementary science, up to the age of 15. This will be only a framework. It is not a question of breaking the old and famous *lycée*. That is broken. It is a question of creating a structure that will at least give the opportunity for creating a general education that will fit the new interests and demands of the vastly increased secondary school population. The old *culture générale*, admirable in many ways as it was, was based on what was thought appropriate for the professional-class youngster in France, as Olive Wykes pointed out long before most French educationists admitted it, in her paper in *Melbourne Studies in Education* for 1961–2.

Our own nineteenth-century notion that the proper basis in general education for a liberal education was in the classics alone looks very odd now. Such an education seems to us to have been more a specialised than a general one. And it was clearly class-related. It is a long time now since we widened the curriculum, in both the independent and the public secondary schools, to include the sciences, but we made a mistake that the French academic secondary schools did not make. We virtually made people choose between one or the other. Limiting our view for the moment to the professional classes, one is struck by the wider general culture of the French, or German or Scandinavian 'technocrat' or technologist than of his English counterpart. Our lawyers, too, have a reputation for integrity that is second to none, but the narrowness of their education contrasts badly with that of their Continental opposite numbers. It is difficult not to connect this with the fact that the education of the *lycée* and the *Gymnasium* has been expected to be more general than ours and that professional education for specific professions is either broader than ours or, as in the United States, does not start until after a first degree has been attained. If it is really rather ridiculous that our early specialising arts students should be so ignorant of the sciences, it is also clear that we shall not liberalise our higher professional and technological studies unless they are preceded by a longer period of general education.

However, our great problem is, so to speak, with the technicians rather than the technologists. It may sound a little patronising to talk of liberalising technical education, but I don't think it will if what is meant is explained. It is not as true as Aristotle and the English nineteenth-century independent schools supposed, that some subjects of study are liberal in themselves and other inevitably illiberal. For one thing, a great deal depends on how they are taught. Latin has often been taught illiberally. Commercial subjects can be taught liberally. What is true is that some studies (history and literature, for example) lend themselves more easily than others (typing and shorthand, to take extreme examples) to a liberal education. Useful skills are to be learned well; there is no point otherwise in attempting them at all. But if for some important purposes they are necessary, though in themselves only skills, they must be studied in a wider educational setting if they are to contribute to liberality of mind.

Most academics seriously under-rate the possibility for liberal study in technical subjects. These are rarely mere skills. I can say this the more freely because I formerly took what seems to me a much too narrow view myself. As a very pure young don I even had grave doubts as to whether engineering was a suitable university study, which seems very silly now. At the London University Institute of Education I was very doubtful about a proposal that commercial subjects should be a recognised course of study and training in some of our colleges of education. But we called for specimen syllabuses, and when I realised that the mere skills could be quite a minor part of a course invoking wider interests I decided that I had been wrong. Again, some academics (however well-read in Plato and Aristotle) think physical education not proper to respectable academic institutions.

The work I have seen in some colleges of education has persuaded me that, rightly conceived, based on the relevant sciences like anatomy and physiology, and related to music, drama, dance and movement, this can provide an excellent and certainly liberal education. Many academics (whose intellectual training has not been such as to prompt them to look at the evidence before making up their minds) suppose physical education, or the art of movement as it now tends to be called, to be nothing but games and physical jerks, just as they suppose domestic science or home economics to be nothing but cooking and sewing.

One difficult problem is to know what to do with so-called liberal studies in art schools and technical colleges. There are technical colleges that have properly developed programmes of study in the humanities and social studies, but many concentrate on what is really technical training of various kinds, just as the art schools concentrate on executive arts and crafts. Tacking on something called liberal studies as a minority subject for young people intent on something else does not seem to have worked out well. The teachers who give such courses find it very difficult to devise a course that makes much sense and they feel themselves extras in institutions whose ethos is not theirs. There is much more hope in colleges that really are colleges of arts and technology. Where this is not so, sooner than have minority time for too general courses in 'liberal studies' I would try to develop a strong if extra-curricular life through musical, dramatic and debating societies, and put on courses that young artisans would see were related to their concerns because they dealt with the social problems of working life.

The really important thing is to broaden technical studies themselves. Let me begin with an almost trivial thing that yet stays in my mind. When I was at school we had a woodwork master, a rightly popular Scottish carpenter, a rough diamond but with a lot of humanity and sense. Once he picked up a piece of wood and asked if anyone knew what kind of wood it was and where it came from. We didn't. He told us what it was and the country the tree grew in. He picked up a piece of chalk and drew a rough map on the bench. 'That,' he said, 'is where this grew and this is the route it took to get here.' I think we understood that woodwork, botany and geography were not separate subjects. Why is cabinet making more 'liberal' than mere carpentry? Not merely because of its precision and polish, but because it raises the work to a level that includes taste and design.

As to technologists, who would normally start with a degree course, Lord Ashby says:[10] 'An undergraduate course in technology which does not include a serious element of humanities and social science is simply not meeting the needs of society'. The work they will do, especially as they assume managerial functions and affect communities of people, will have this wider human and social setting and it is perilous to neglect it.

Two things, then, above all make the more liberal man. One is this capacity to take the larger view. The other is interest in the basic knowledge, as it were for its own sake. It is finding the answer to the question 'why?' and not being content with the question 'how?' that releases one of the

important elements that can liberalise vocational and technical or technological education.

If we could press harder for these things and above all never forget the
need of men and women to find satisfaction beyond drudgery and beyond
the bread and butter necessities then the ordinary man would find within
his reach the liberal education that was once the privilege of a minority.
Bunyan the tinker and the visionary understood this. In our more secular
society it is a liberal education that can enable us to raise our eyes, though
we still have to handle the muckrake, from the straws, the sticks and the
dust on the floor.

Chapter 4

A Controversial Question: Compulsory Religion in the Public School System[1]

There is one kind of commonsense that is not sensible, the kind that always seeks some comfortable halfway house when a question ought to be thought out clearly and a decision of principle made. In such cases the halfway house is rarely comfortable for long: the refusal to think the matter through merely leads to a piling up of discomfort on discomfort. Such, it seems to me, is the state we are in now about compulsory religious education in the public schools. (The term used in the 1944 Act is 'religious instruction', and I use the term 'religious education' in deference to those who would like to liberalise it though they do not wish to end compulsion.)

In dealing with the problem of schools that are religious foundations we tend to pride ourselves on our commonsense in this country. It is said that we have avoided the bitter divisions that rent French society for so long; and there is an arguable case for maintaining this, though I am not entirely certain of it. But that is not what I would like to discuss in this chapter. Nor, although I shall say something about religion as a school subject, am I really discussing religion. The problem I would like to discuss is that of compulsory religion in schools that belong to the whole public in a multi-belief and increasingly non-belief society. For the sake of candour I should say that my personal view of religions is that in their theistic aspect they are myth-systems through which some of the best, and some of the worst, sides of human nature have expressed themselves. But I would hope that since my main point is not about religion but about fairness in a multi-belief society, adherents of one or other of our religions would agree with me as much as those who adhere to none. Charles Kingsley, that very militant churchman, expressed the view when public education came in with the 1870 Act that in an increasingly secular age teaching in these schools should be secular and the clergy left to teach about God.[2]

If Kingsley felt a century ago that we were increasingly a secular society he would have no doubt as to what our society is now. To describe it as a Christian country is true in the sense that this has been our tradition and true in the sense that Christianity is still for many purposes official. But in two more important respects it would be misleading. There is a much stronger representation than there used to be of other religions: we have long had a Jewish community, but now there are appreciable numbers of

Muslims, Hindus, Sikhs and Buddhists. And in Kingsley's time we were very much a Protestant country. Since Catholic Emancipation the Roman Catholic community has come more into the main stream of English life. Again, we are much more secular, in the sense that the proportion of people who take seriously the observances and adhere in any precise sense to the beliefs of any religion has fallen greatly. How you count what adherence to a religious community means affects any statistical result you will get, and this is particularly so of the very large middle group of people who hardly ever go to a church (perhaps only for a wedding or a funeral) and who might, if asked, say they supposed there was a God but who would answer in the negative if pressed on further matters of belief. Mr Geoffrey Gorer, as reported in *The Times* of 29 April 1965, found that of 359 people he questioned only 11 held orthodox beliefs about an after-life and a quarter stated firmly that they did not believe in a life after death. The number of people who not only tacitly assent when a minister of religion tells them that God is a Trinity, one in three and three in one, but who have any sort of understanding of so puzzling a doctrine must be quite small. It is likely that the proportions found by Mr Gorer ten years ago would be smaller still now. Other sample polls, though less sensationally, show the same trend. Professor Niblett, a Christian himself, gave one of his books the title, *Christian Education in a Secular Society*. We are not fully secular yet, but for all but official purposes that is now a fairly accurate description of our society. What is certain is that we are no longer a single Protestant belief society and that as between believers in any religion and non-believers we are now very mixed.

This being so, and if we were starting public education afresh, the point would be made strongly that schools belonging to all of us and for the children of all of us must be neutral in this matter, in common fairness. But, it is said, we are not starting afresh. Historically Christianity has been the religion of all of us, except for the smallest minority. It is part of the English heritage and tradition. It is also (though only since 1944) a compulsory part of the curriculum. Why be doctrinaire? Surely no one can object to a fair and tolerant presentation of Christianity in the schools, especially as there is a conscience clause allowing children and teachers to opt out?

It is true that some parents with no beliefs of their own do tolerate this. But here we have run into the disadvantages of the halfway house. On the one hand an increasing number of parents feel offended that their children have inculcated into them beliefs for which they see no justification and that they actively reject. (I noticed an indignant protest about this from Mr Harold Pinter the dramatist, and for one who is stirred to writing to the papers about it there must be many more who feel strongly but do not go that far.) Teachers are increasingly protesting, too. I heard one of them on a recent BBC programme say quite simply that they should not have to teach, or at least give observed assent, to what they believed not to be true.

Perhaps because heads of schools and teachers in charge of religious education are aware of these strong feelings, and often are sympathetic to them, they water down the religious education that is given and turn the statutory 'act of worship' and the RI period into something that a serious religious person would not recognise as such at all. Practice varies, and so much that generalisation is difficult. But this watering down has gone so far that some Christians insist that all teachers involved be convinced Christians, which in the present state of opinion is impossible, if only because of the numbers involved. Some Christians realise that all this, from their own point of view, is doing more harm than good. So much for the commonsense halfway house.

For a good long time, indeed until the last decade or two, the weight of tradition in England was such that there was nothing like equality of respect for believers and non-believers as groups in society, though ours being on the whole a tolerant country the feelings of individuals, once made known, were normally treated with courtesy. Many Christians still allow themselves to be quickly offended if doubt about their beliefs is expressed with any sharpness, but do not realise that their assumption that decent people of course share their outlook is offensive to those who do not.

Let me give two examples, one more extreme than the other. Once, at a meeting about religious education in schools, I expressed myself with some irony about the idea of the 'virgin birth', recalling that this was the sort of myth accretion one might expect in accounts of men-gods and heroes. Most thinking Christians would agree with this, but one rather eminent person present accused me of being arrogant, and I realised that I had touched him somewhere too deep for normal commonsense to apply. Believers in fact assert that this story is true whenever they recite the creeds and he did not see that those parents who did not believe it had every reason to complain of the arrogance of those who fastened it on their young in the public schools.

Take a more central example. The affirmation of the Resurrection is that a man, who was also the Son of God, lived on the earth, was crucified and died, and after three days in hell rose from the dead. If, never having heard of such a belief, we met it among a newly discovered people on a South Sea island we should feel it to be a pretty improbable story. Indeed, the analogy is curiously close: the 'cargo cult' of some people in the western Pacific, that a boat will return laden with all the things they could desire, as the Americans came in the war, is smiled at by all educated people. But children in the schools are led to believe that the Christian Resurrection actually happened; and by happened I mean happened. It is not spoken of as a myth, like the return of Persephone in the spring. The way in which the two stories are presented is quite different. Those who believe in the Resurrection have every right to express their belief, but those who do not are equally entitled to express their disbelief. Why should the schools give every official opportunity to one and no official opportunity to the other? If the public schools were enjoined by law to engage in propaganda for atheism there would be an outcry from Christians, and rightly so. Christian conformists find it hard to understand that non-Christian parents may be equally offended with the present official bias, and with equal right. Now the number of parents who do not believe in the truth of the Resurrection story is growing and the gap between them and the official doctrine of the schools is widening.

There was a halfway house in which people thought they might be comfortable: no teaching 'of' any set of beliefs but teaching 'about' various kinds of belief and attitude. But this apparently is no longer available. The new (1974) agreed syllabus of the Local Education Authority of the City of Birmingham, which attempted to do this, was blocked. Counsel gave it as his opinion that when the 1944 Act said 'religious instruction', it meant that, and not mere discussion 'about' religious and other ideologies.[3] It probably did; but the hope was that the meaning might be broadened in practice and dispute avoided. But the halfway house seems to have been built on sand. Reluctant though the British public is to face an issue of principle and to apply genuine commonsense instead of its halfway house spurious imitation, that it will have to do so is increasingly likely.

A publication some years ago of the Christian Institute of Education[4] recognised that prayers in school would often not be supported by prayers at home. It said: 'It is the sincerity and integrity of the teacher that will surmount this hurdle.' But suppose the sincerity and the integrity of the teacher impel him not to engage in such exercises? Are sincerity and integrity to be respected only in Christian believers? In a population with a great diversity of views about religion, and probably now a majority of non-believers, it is unlikely that there will emerge a corps of teachers for all the schools who are zealous practising Christians. A young teacher wrote about this in the organ of the National Union of Teachers, *The Teacher* (28 February 1964). He said of the morning assembly for the 'act of worship':

Such an assembly necessitates some reverence, even if only simulated. The enforced quiet is the responsibility of the adult teachers sprinkled among the children, waiting for the entry of the officers each morning.

What worries me is that I am required to do this every morning in defiance of any conscience I might have. Maybe it is because I am new that I chafe at the hypocrisy required of me. I must police children and mumble hymns and prayers, without believing at all in either the ceremony itself or the wider implications of it. Nobody seems to care that there is any hypocrisy.

He says he knows you may contract out, but that if you raise the question you are put off with talk about the value of assemblies and it is assumed that, like playground duty, this is one of the things all the staff should do. He asks in how many schools this freedom to contract out has any substance. 'And,' he adds, 'we have our references to think of.'

This is of course like the conscience clause for the parents of children who do not want them to attend the 'acts of worship' or the 'RI' period. It is asking a great deal of a child to agree to be singled out as a member of a non-conforming minority; most such parents feel it is better to do nothing about it. It seems to me that those who want to retain the compulsion of the 1944 Act incur a very serious moral responsibility and that they are in a position that cannot be defended.

There is a kind of blandness about their statements that is amazing when one thinks that the schools really aren't their private preserve. The publication to which I have referred says on page 39, discussing the morning 'act of worship':

It is imperative that this act of worship be planned and conducted carefully and with conviction, and that it be regarded by all as of over-riding importance in the life of the school, because the quality of that life is profoundly influenced by it. Above all, the impression must be avoided that the service is a mere minor appendage to a routine assembly of the whole school. The important thing to remember is that every school assembly is an avenue for the activity of God.

This is indeed mandatory. It commands teachers that they must believe something. The act of worship must be so regarded by *all*. To insist that all teachers, parents and children in a multi-belief society must share and express the same beliefs is to live in an unreal world. It is also to be intolerant. It implies that those teachers who do not wish to be active participants in such official services have less right than others in a school. This attitude to teachers in schools is quite different from anything one finds in universities, where the opinions of the teachers and students as to religion are their own business. Anyone who has worked in a university institute of education, in contact with both worlds, is made very conscious of the difference. There can surely be no disagreement as to which attitude is the proper one.

What actually happens in the schools varies greatly. In some there is not an act of worship every morning. In some there is nothing that in any direct way is 'religious instruction'. There is reading from other books than the Bible, talk about other religions than Christianity, even a turning of the RI period into a period for moral education (which is not really right, for moral education, as I have said in my first chapter, should have its own autonomy and not be 'closed' by being conducted under religious auspices). It would be rash to assume that this is the general picture. In any case the general official ethos remains that of the beliefs of one section only of the parents. And there are serious difficulties about a supposed 'open' approach, hopeful though one might once have been that the objectionable clause of the Act could just drop out of practice without formal repeal.

In honest logic we cannot reconcile an 'open' approach, that gives no more official approval to one kind of attitude than to another, with the 1944 Act. The hope of the halfway house always depended on people's refraining from pressing that point, and since the Birmingham case it is clear that this is not likely to happen. There is no doubt that when the 1944 Act speaks of 'worship', though it lacks the moral courage to add the necessary predicate (for you can't just 'worship', you must worship something or someone), it means the worship of God as understood by Christians. If we stick to this we are confronted not with an open question but with an answer.

Doctrines may be literally or liberally interpreted. But making allowance for this I should not have thought there was all that room for doubt as to what the basic beliefs of Christianity were. Archbishop Beck, writing in the *Times Educational Supplement* for 16 April 1965, stated the essential Christian doctrine with complete clarity. He said that the fundamental truth is that 'God is the creator and father of all mankind' and that 'God has revealed his purpose for us in the Incarnation of his Son, Jesus Christ'. Surely any Christian, if he were instructed in his religion, would say that these were his basic beliefs. I would have thought that the doctrine of the Incarnation would need to be held to include that of the Resurrection, and that since the Council of Nicaea a Christian must be a Trinitarian and not an Arian. But there is no need to press these things from the present point of view. But can a person who is open in his mind as to whether there is a God be described as a Christian? Is the existence of a God, as Archbishop Beck with undoubted historical warrant uses the term, an open or a decided question? The difficulty is that if it is not open very little is.

There are a few Christian educationists who would allow it to be, mostly to be found in university posts rather than in the Establishment of any of the churches. But the Rev. Allan Wainwright, the Education Secretary of the British Council of Churches, wrote in the same issue of the *Times Educational Supplement*:

> When we remember that most children have no significant participation in any specific Christian heritage and that home, far from countering the pressures of society, acts as a reinforcement to them, it is clear that an inducting type of religious education is quite inappropriate.
>
> On the contrary, the only justification for the inclusion of religious teaching in every school is that the issues with which it deals are of such importance that every individual ought to have the opportunity to get to grips with them: more, that all pupils should be faced with facts and ideas which force them in their turn to ask ultimate questions and seek for answers.
>
> Not to ask such questions is to be less than fully human: but in an open society such as ours, there can be no guarantee that the orthodox answers will either be reached, or if reached, accepted.

This is 'open', and a non-Christian parent would infinitely prefer such an attitude to one that implies that the 'orthodox' answers are the only possible right ones. If this were the attitude officially encouraged we should in fact have moved away from the relevant clause in the Act to something like the situation in Sweden, where the purpose is to explain about religions, not to induct into any one of them. No view would have special official approval. This is not at all what the 1944 Act had in mind. And I very much doubt whether it is what goes on in any but a small minority of schools.

The more general position, put with perhaps a shade more of unsuspecting candour than usual, was that stated by a headmistress in the *Times Educational Supplement* for 12 April 1963.

> What is the goal of the religious instruction specialist? It is to achieve in each young person a sense of the reality of God, and some experience of worship. It is to instruct him in the faith and answer some of his intellectual doubts and difficulties.

There is no hesitancy about that. It is indoctrination pure and simple. It begs every question that should be open. It does not seek answers; it claims to know them in advance.

But where do those people stand who would disavow any attempt at indoctrination and yet keep religious education as a compulsory thing? Rather few, I think would go the whole way towards making all questions in it open. If they did they would have to agree (and I know one teacher who has argued this strongly) that an atheist, properly versed in his subject, would be just as fitted to take a period of religious education as a convinced Christian. Somehow I think that that is unlikely to win general acceptance unless the purpose of these periods is explicitly changed.

The term 'indoctrination' is a difficult one, though I sometimes think not quite as difficult as some who gain from the difficulty would make out. We mean by it a persistent and explicit endeavour to make someone accept a belief as true without fair consideration of alternatives. What goes with it is usually an attempt, through group pressure, to make those who do not accept it feel a sense of guilt. Many public schools do not now indoctrinate in this full sense. But short of this – whatever name one uses for it – there is a conditioning deriving from the obvious special position of official approval given to one set of beliefs.

For a teacher there is one very simple test. If a boy or girl leaves school as a reasonably responsible person, intellectually and morally, but with different opinions (not necessarily different basic standards of conduct) from those of his teacher, will the teacher feel that he has failed in his task? The teacher who understands what liberal education is will answer with a firm 'No'. The proselytiser, the surrogate priest in the school, will normally feel that he must have failed. I would only add that some priests and ministers in schools will be philosophically tolerant, though I think they will be sad about it as the teacher who understands what liberal education is will not.

This is the root difficulty about religious education in schools. It was well put by that admirable columnist, writing under his pen-name Peter Quince, in *The Teacher* (7 December 1962). He said that in an age of appeals to mass credulity by advertisers and propagandists of all kinds, teachers are bound to encourage children

> . . . to seek out the motives behind unsupported statements and to question the authority on which they are made. . . . They feel they must

warn children that there never has been a time when it was so important
not to take statements on trust but to examine everything critically in the
light of logic and tried experience. But the schools cannot speak with two
voices. They cannot teach children how to look at life critically in lessons
on civics and current affairs, and urge them to be uncritical in religious
instruction.

This disparity between the intellectual standard of religious education
and that of other subjects in the school is bound to worry those who are
serious about education. At a meeting with religious educationists I once
quoted another passage from the publication of the Institute of Christian
Education to which I have referred. On page 13 we are told: 'The child
who has seen the emerging wonder of a daffodil planted deep in the dark
earth – a dry, lifeless-looking thing – now triumphantly bursting with bright
colour in the springtime has learned more of wonder, of life and resurrection, than the child who is told "God makes the pretty flowers".' The
dishonest word here is 'resurrection', as we realise a few pages later when
we find that included in the list of things that should be taught is the
Resurrection, this time *the* Resurrection. The way has been prepared. Now
to suggest that there is a parallel here, that because daffodils come up in
the spring we must believe in the story of the Resurrection, is not treating
either children or their teachers with respect. The flowers that bloom in the
spring have nothing to do with the case. I do not think such laughable
looseness would appear in recommendations to teachers for any other
subject in the schools.

Now when I quoted this passage I was told that I wasn't being fair,
because this was meant for quite small children. But this is when habits of
thought begin to be formed. Another story in the book is of a little girl who
tried to telephone Jesus to thank him for the recovery of her mother from
illness, and this was praised as truly praying. I might have commented on it
in the light of a sermon I heard Dean Inge preach to adults in the University
Church at Cambridge – after the Bidding Prayer had been said, of course –
on the foolishness of petitionary prayer. But the excuse is not good enough.

Of course one speaks simply to young children. But in all other subjects
we do so in such a way that they will not have to unlearn anything when
they are older. If we speak in parables we do so in parables that do not
falsify the facts or induce bad mental habits. Why has the parable of the
Good Samaritan had such a hold on men's minds? Because though it
simplifies (the relations between hostile human groups raise some complicated problems) it does not falsify. Its essential message is right.

The difficulty about Bible teaching – and that is what RI has largely
been, and often still is – is that to understand the Bible one needs the aid
of many kinds of scholarship. Only so can we know what the words meant
to the writers who used them in the setting of their own times, and considerable learning and insight are needed to render them in our terms. If
you try to teach the Bible as unique truth to young children you are driven
back to fundamentalism, unless of course you treat its stories as a mixture

of fact and myth like the stories children hear from Greece and Rome. But Christians could hardly agree to that.

The relationship between fact and fantasy in young children is subtly different from that in a mature person. Nevertheless if you make a statement of fact to children they understand well enough what realm of discourse you are in. If you want to make an 'as if' or 'let's pretend' statement to children their suspension of disbelief may be different from an adult's, the imaginary may be more intensely real to them, but they understand whether you are telling them a fairy story or not. The most they do sometimes is to ask, to make sure. If you are telling them a Greek myth they may ask if Apollo really existed, but I know of no child who has been converted to a belief in the Greek gods because we tell these stories of them. But when teachers tell them stories from the Bible the implications conveyed are quite different. What does a teacher say when a child asks if water really can be turned into wine? Sophisticated explanations will not serve. The child wants a yes or a no. Most parents now would say no. In short, if you are talking in the realm of historical fact, the story is not to be taken as true. How many teachers of the religious education period will say that quite simply and clearly? And if they themselves think it did happen what public criterion of truth do they use? It must be a public one, for in a class they are in a public situation.

Now it is fashionable in sophisticated religious circles to dismiss this kind of comment as terribly crude. Whether that be so or not it is what a child means when he says, 'Did that really happen?', and it seems to me that children deserve an honest answer in the perfectly legitimate terms in which they ask the question. In fact whole areas of religious belief (from witchcraft to – except apparently for some bishops – literal possession by devils) have dropped out of religious 'truth' that must be accepted by true believers. So have such beliefs as that God did make the sun stand still so that Joshua could win a battle. The reason they have dropped out is that the child's test has been applied. In what we ordinarily call matters of fact, scientific or historical, most people now come to a conclusion about what is said in the Bible on scientific or historical grounds, not those of revelation. And many Christians say that this can be done, without their giving up what they feel to be the essentials of Christianity. But in schools this position has not been generally reached (and it is a rather sophisticated one). Their religious teaching is regressive rather than progressive.

In the number of the *Times Educational Supplement* from which I have already quoted, Mr Norman Bull, of St Luke's College, Exeter, writes: 'The incessant "is it true" of the older junior is the opportunity to show how truth, far too immense a concept to be limited to mere historicity – though there are those who propagate such a heresy – is mediated in different forms, each conveying truth in its own right.' Not what is 'mere historicity'? Does Mr Bull mean that he can assert that something is historically true when as sober historians we should seriously doubt it? Does he mean that we are not to apply historical criteria to what purport to be historical statements? How does one distinguish between religious statements that have the form of historical statements but really belong to another mode of truth existing in its own right, and real historical statements? When Gibbon in a famous chapter pointed out that although there were many very competent chroniclers and observers at the time none seems to have noticed that darkness covered the earth for some hours at the Crucifixion, was he indulging in 'mere historicity'? If that tiresome junior asked Mr Bull if it was true that darkness did cover the earth at this time, the sense in which he would be using the word 'true' would be perfectly plain, and there would be only one honest answer: 'No, so far as we can tell, it did not.' It is this reluctance to use the standards of validity that we try so hard to inculcate in all other school lessons that makes compulsory religious education so uncomfortable a bedfellow in the comfortable halfway house. Surely the sensible thing would be to recognise that religious people do ultimately believe as a matter of faith and that this is not in a public realm coextensive with our whole society, and that religious instruction had better therefore be left to the homes and the clergy that want it. At any rate it is quite wrong that it should be compulsory, with one view, and not others, given official blessing.

This conclusion is reinforced by the present sad state of moral education in the schools. The halfway house here is to let it happen in the wake of religious education. I have already made the case for moral education in its own right. Treating it as a concomitant of a religious education in whose sanctions many young people do not now believe has proved ineffective. Once more the halfway house kind of 'commonsense' has led to a breakdown. There are situations in which real commonsense demands a clean break, not a compromise.

PART II COMMONSENSE AND CONCEPTS

Chapter 5

Facts, Beliefs and Values

So far we have been considering the place of commonsense in making decisions about the curriculum. Whatever general ideas this may involve it is essentially a matter of practice. Any theory about it has to stand the tests of a working theory. I would now like to ask a more difficult question: how far has commonsense a place in more markedly theoretical thinking, in particular in the elucidation of the concepts we use in discussing education?

Such concepts have been analysed, often without agreed conclusions, by philosophers. Those of us who are not philosophers by training have also to think critically about them. I wish to argue that there is a considerable area where we should not be afraid to argue from general good sense, no doubt supplemented by such specialist reading as we can manage; and that in particular it is important for teachers and student teachers to bring their own good sense to bear even though the writings of specialist philosophers, sociologists and psychologists may seem frighteningly recondite. This is a slightly dangerous assertion, for I am not saying that we do not need such specialised studies. I am aware, for example, that if I use a word like 'perception' I shall trigger off all sorts of complicated questions in the mind of any philosopher or psychologist who may read this part of this book. In some places I may refer to such questions. I can only hope that my references are valid and that I do not ignore too many such questions altogether. But I am very sure that refined analyses are less necessary in some places than in others and I want to stake a claim for informed good sense over a large part of the ground.

Take an example that will form part of what follows in this chapter. There can be much argument as to what we mean when we say, 'That is a fact'. But there is a level of discourse where the question, 'Is that a fact?' is perfectly legitimate and occasions no confusion between questioner and questioned. Again, there has been endless argument as to the meaning of the concept Truth but there are very large areas of discussion where we are all speaking within the framework of the correspondence theory of truth (does a proposition correspond to what we perceive of external reality?) and no one has any doubt about this. Analysis that goes further than this may be important and often is; but if such subtleties are imperfectly mastered, or worse are used casuistically, they may confuse rather than clarify. That is why, though we all know the pitfalls in apparently common-sense explanations, we must fall back on our commonsense. It is at least a correction to specialist fashion.

This is the question I wish to explore in this part of this book; and I begin with three concepts that we all invoke, both in general and in educational discussion: facts, beliefs and values.

Schools have always been expected to furnish the young with factual information. They are also expected to transmit the values of their society. And most schools are committed to some system of beliefs, political or religious. In all three of these realms there is controversy at the present time.

This is obvious so far as values and beliefs are concerned. But there are also controversies about facts. What is assumed to be factually correct in a textbook in the Soviet Union may be challenged in a Western country, and vice versa. Does this raise the question, 'What is a fact?' or only the question, 'Is that a fact?' The disagreement as to whether something is a fact very often makes us ask how far beliefs and values are involved in selecting the facts that we decide to teach. Ought schools to indoctrinate the young with any beliefs not grounded in facts that those not holding such beliefs would also agree were facts? Can we avoid a measure of indoctrination? If we did what would be the consequence to society? Should we welcome an extension of factual knowledge that makes us modify cherished beliefs, as forty years ago Ruth Benedict's *Patterns of Culture* led people to think that morality was much more a matter of geography and less of absolutes than they had supposed? Again, cramming the young with facts may be at the expense of comprehension of principles or inimical to the life of the imagination. How do we give factual information its proper place without these possible bad consequences?

These are important questions. Are we entitled to discuss them and give our views without having first decided what we mean by a 'fact'? There are some discussions where such initial clarification is indispensable. If you have not first thought out what you mean by a 'right', argument about who has what rights in education will only spread confusion. I do not think that at a certain practical level this is so with a word like 'fact', because at that level there is no misunderstanding about it. I am not saying that it may not be good to penetrate beyond the commonsense level.[1] On the contrary, the discussions among philosophers about facts, sense data, and so on, are important. But it is not necessary to have read *Sense and Sensibilia* to discuss any of the questions about facts in education that I have mentioned in my last paragraph. 'Let Austin have his swynke to him reserved.'

This is a point of some importance because there are people who like, in Dr Johnson's words, to perplex the confines of distinction to buttress a position by mystification. I was once at a discussion meeting with scientists of considerable standing. In support of something I had said I appealed to the facts. 'Ah,' said one of them, 'but I don't think there is such a thing as a fact.' The short answer to him would have been that in that case what he had just said was not a fact either. Or, putting it differently, what he had just said was equivalent to saying that there are no true propositions. Since he himself must therefore have believed that the proposition he had just enunciated was false there was no need for further argument.

I think I know what he had in mind, unless he was getting in an oblique defence of his religion. The statement that a table is a solid object can be reduced by a physicist to an account of a table in terms of atoms and particles that make it seem far from solid. You do not disprove this by hitting the table, hurting your fist and demonstrating that it is only too solid, any more than Dr Johnson disproved Berkeley by kicking the stone. Nevertheless the statement that a table is solid is perfectly valid in its own sphere of discourse, that of ordinary speech. It is grounded in the distinction between a table that we call solid and something liquid or gaseous on which my interlocutor would not have wished you to set his dinner. I am afraid my interlocutor was being rather clever-silly. For people normally understand quite well the context in which something is said: the context is part of the meaning. At our level of discourse when this red herring was thrown in nobody was confused by the use of the word fact. Confusion comes when something is said, not necessarily untrue but inappropriate and diversionary. At that point it seems to me that the sometimes too modest layman must stand up and insist that the criterion he has advanced (in this case, 'Does it fit the facts?') is a perfectly proper one in the context. The tactic to which I have taken exception can be used as a debating ploy, or it can be used innocently by people who are themselves victims of it. It is not philosophy of any kind. It is merely bad semantics.

Although, therefore, we are not to be bullied out of the use of a word like 'fact' when it is necessary and not misleading, nevertheless understanding that at other levels of discourse it may be a blunt instrument is salutary. Thus, unless one believes that there is an ideal Cow (of which particular cows are imperfect examples) one will understand that to speak of The Cow is to use classificatory shorthand. Without this device of language and thought we should be precluded from making any significant general statements. We know that there are cows of many kinds and colours, but they vary about a norm; and The Cow is the term we use for this norm. We do not perceive The Cow directly: it is a mental construct or, if you prefer that way of putting it, its reality is in the world of ideas.

Some languages do not have as many general classificatory terms as ours. They may have no word for, say, white, but many words for different shades of white; or no one word for cow, or yam, but words for different kinds of cow or yam. Their language is appropriate to a culture that is different from ours. But language is not just a neutral medium through which we express thoughts that would be precisely the same in another language. In one sense the particular language we use structures the account we give of things, one might almost say modifies the way we habitually see them. I say in one sense because it does not necessarily follow that when experiencing a different cultural situation a speaker of such a 'primitive' language could not make the distinctions or the generalisations appropriate to that culture. We may see things differently through our language habits but yet be capable of sharing each other's perceptions. This is an important point to remember for Western teachers of children whose mother tongues are of the kind I have referred to.

We use the word 'fact' to indicate a reality we have perceived and that we assume others can perceive. A fact and a private hallucination are different. We assume that others – not necessarily at first glance, but if they observe carefully – will agree that what we see as part of external reality will be so for them also. This works quite well for ordinary purposes, and there is no misunderstanding about it so long as we remember that what I have called first perceptions may differ.

Our mechanisms of perception are selective, and we do not all select in the same way. Some writers have argued that they are so selective that they reflect our personal values, what may be for us most significant in a situation. This in part is why two equally normal and honest people may see the same incident in different lights and report on it differently. But although, if the evaluation has been simultaneous with the perception, it may be difficult to come back on it for re-examination, there is considerable hope that we can get two people who have 'seen' something differently to agree as to what are the facts and what the subjective interpretations they have put upon them. This is the basis of finding a measure of consensus as to the 'facts' of a situation.

All this is of great importance for education. Like so much else in our social intercourse, education depends upon successful communication between persons. The qualifications I have just noted would seem to recommend a certain patience, a readiness not to be too immediately sweeping, when we say 'That is a fact' and someone else says, 'But I don't think it is'. When that happens one has to see whether the difference is due to a remediable failure on the part of one of the persons (so that he will come round to agree with the other) or to a basic incapacity. This is the essence of explanatory teaching.

There is a kind of tone that is too peremptory – 'These are the facts, and if you can't grasp that so much the worse for you.' But this is quite different from maintaining that there are no facts, that there cannot be any true propositions. I am arguing for the recognition of the commonsense level of discourse, not for aggressiveness where perceptions may be different and care needed to find out why. This is one guide to the difference between a good and a poor teacher. It is important to distinguish between sensitiveness to personal differences, which we need, and sophistry, which we must detect and reject.

In speaking of facts I have used the phrase 'true propositions' and have implied that there are true propositions. The commonsense comment is immediate: of course there are. If there were not, no human communication would be possible beyond the grunts and growls of approval and disapproval. Yet the word 'truth' has been the subject of much disputation, much of it of course serious, but some of it obfuscatory because people have not made clear the level at which they are speaking. The word has various shades of meaning. One of the great difficulties is the legitimacy or otherwise of the use of the word to indicate not only accuracy of information but moral or aesthetic satisfaction. When Keats said that Beauty was Truth, Truth Beauty, was he making the remark of an uneducated man or expressing something profound? For the purpose of my argument here I do not need to go into these questions, though it would be imperceptive not to mention them. The point I wish to make is simple: for most of our ordinary purposes we mean by 'true', corresponding to an external reality we perceive, and this is a perfectly satisfactory mental framework for deciding many questions, though there are other questions for which it would not be. To get answers to questions like 'Is it true that you were at home on Friday morning instead of being at work?' or 'Is it true that there are many children in the world who do not go to school at all?' you do not need to ask what we mean by perception, still less what is the nature of Reality. Some of the confusion of thinking about beliefs in particular seems to me to arise because people will invoke questions like these when they are not pertinent and are quite unnecessary and therefore diversionary. I am not saying that they are always so.

We can for the present leave open the question whether there is a realm of experience not grounded in sense experience. The realm of discourse I am referring to is of the kind when we say that there are two apples in a basket and someone else says there are three. We decide the question not by discussing whether there is an ideal Apple, nor by investigating the physico-chemical structure of apples, but by looking and counting. And the phrase we use – not needing any further definition for our well-understood present purpose – is, 'Is it true that there are two apples in the basket, or are there three?'.

We do not need to ask whether the correspondence theory of truth is adequate. We use it, rightly agreeing that for this kind of purpose it is. A Platonist who says there are two apples in the basket and a non-Platonist who says there are three both make their claim within the theory. They are both saying, 'Is it a fact that there are two or are there three?'. If we did not use the word fact we should only have to find some longer and less convenient locution to say the same thing. If the Platonist said there only appeared to be three apples, sense perception giving us only a shadow of reality, or if the non-Platonist raised doubts about the physical structure of the apples, we should say they were evading the question. And we should be right.

As I have just hinted, this point is important in its bearings on matters of belief. 'Belief' is an odd word. Beliefs, especially in religion and politics, are apt to be held passionately. Yet when we say we believe something we normally mean that we think something is so but cannot demonstrate it certainly – if at all. If we have just looked into the basket, counted and found there are two apples, we say 'I know there are two'. If we say only that we believe there are two we are making a less confident statement. We think there are two, feel tolerably sure of it, but are really not 100 per cent certain.

Now when someone tells us that he believes something we usually ask him what are the grounds for his belief, a question that goes with the correspondence theory of truth. If he convinces us that he has good grounds for his belief, though not conclusive ones, we think he is answering us reasonably. If he cannot give us fairly good grounds then, unless we ourselves are already within his belief system, we are apt to dismiss his beliefs as in the realm of mere desires, or fantasy, or superstition. When we ask for grounds we mean evidence or a reasonable deduction from it. If we did not have this kind of criterion we should lack (as has often been pointed out) any way of choosing between one belief and another. 'Credo quia impossible est' has the short-term advantage of ruling all evidence or reason out of court, but the long-term disadvantage of leaving us with no criterion in a world where there is a great variety of beliefs, some of them incompatible with others.

We can do something to disentangle all this. When someone tells us that he has a certain belief we can fairly ask him how far this relates to matters he would agree came within the correspondence conception of truth, and then test to see whether there are the correspondences he has supposed. This is not an easy point to press, although there are honest people in every belief system who would be uneasy if they claimed as fact what was not fact. Deep feelings are commonly involved. Moreover, there are various ways, some more respectable than others, by which adherents of belief systems can reconcile to themselves public assertions that they have more than a little doubt about. One very persuasive argument goes: if you undermine a belief system by suggesting that some of the propositions that support it are not justified by the evidence, you also undermine the moral values, or the social purposes, associated with the belief system; and this you would not want to do. You may do public harm to satisfy your personal conscience. Entertain your doubts by all means, but privately. Thus in religion there are sophisticated Christians who do not believe in a physical hell and sophisticated Hindus who must have doubts about reincarnation, but if belief in hell or in reincarnation makes ordinary people live more morally for fear of what will happen to them in an after-life, is not that better than that the bonds of society should be weakened? Or in politics, there must be sophisticated Communists who do not think that all painting since Cubism is decadent or that parliamentary democracy in England is like what Dickens described in the Eatonswill election, and there must be opponents of Communism who notice with some approval the liberation of the energies of the people that can accompany it (for instance in China); but is either kind of person right in saying this so publicly that in the one case he weakens the people's will to defend the Communist society or in the other jeopardises free society by being 'soft on Communism'?

Such representations are plausible and not easily to be countered within a belief system to which you honestly adhere. The reasonably modest individual (not St Joan but the kind of person the Inquisitor thought she should be) hesitates to set himself up against a whole church or a whole regime by challenging the factual basis of their assertions. He feels that he may indeed weaken it, and that he does not want to.

The answers to this kind of representation are three. First, candour about the truth of propositions involved in a belief system, so far from weakening it may strengthen it. It may help to purge it of matter (often an historical accretion) that is not essential and is bound sooner or later to bring it into disrepute. Whether it does so or not depends largely on whether the criticism it invites is necessarily radical. Secondly there is the pragmatic argument that once the factual evidence against a given assertion gets known its defenders will be seen in a bad light if they rather stupidly persist in defending what is palpably not true. But people within a belief system who do have private doubts about some of its assertions are apt not to raise such questions themselves. When controversy has started they may be wise to give up positions that they feel cannot really be defended. These two reasons are, of course, closely related.

The third argument is the fundamental one: that an ideology resting on propositions that that can be shown to be untrue is not worthy of an honest man's support. Let allowance be made for not being a stiff-necked person, for the recognition of traditions as valuable even though they enshrine statements that we should not accept literally, there still comes a point where an honest man must speak up for what he believes to be the truth. Unfortunately this is much easier to see from outside than from inside a given system of beliefs.

This problem affects everyone, but it particularly affects teachers in a public system of education. If their society includes in its values the nourishing of a critical spirit of inquiry they will enjoy greater freedom than teachers in a less liberal regime. But being both individual persons with their integrity and at the same time public trustees they have a problem that may at any time become acute. Let me illustrate this first with a rather simple, and apparently even minor, example.

I saw in a textbook in a Moscow school the statement that in the United Kingdom all the means of production are privately owned. This is not true – the coal mines and the railways, for instance, are owned by the nation – and it is a little shocking to find such an elementary mis-statement in an official textbook that must have been exposed to 'vetting' in several places. It would probably not occur to a boy or girl in the class to question the statement. England is a capitalist country; a capitalist country is one in which the means of production are privately owned; therefore it would be natural to suppose that in England they all are. Why did not the textbook get the facts right? It could have taken the line that in a capitalist country some industry may be in public hands without altering the fundamentally capitalist nature of the society and the economy. But some official looking over the textbook might have felt that would be a little tricky. It might open the way to the consideration of the policy of a mixed economy, even of Social Democratic gradual evolution to socialism. Better leave the passage in, though it was not literally true. The teacher might have been able safely to correct the mis-statement of fact and say it did not affect the main point. But in such societies one has to be very careful. After all, the textbooks authorised are very official documents. But everyone outside the USSR and its allies would say that this defence really will not do.

As we have seen, some of the most difficult problems come within the area of religion. In England, where there is compulsory religious instruction, teachers often have a difficult time with their consciences: either they give public assent, or even recommendation, to what they doubt, or they fail in a school duty. Most systems of religious belief include propositions of a factual kind, involving the structure and origin of the universe and the earth, the history of mankind, even matters of medicine. How far are these to be taken as true (in the correspondence sense by which they would be tested in the sciences or in historical studies) and how far as myth, however interesting and perhaps illuminating?

It is said that the controversies associated with Bishop Colenso of Natal in the mid-nineteenth century originated in a simple question from one of his Zulu followers.[2] He was translating the account of the origin of the earth and its living things given in the Book of Genesis when the Zulu said, 'But is this true?'. He meant: did it happen like that, historically? Colenso was too honest to think he could avoid this question by devices about truth and 'higher' truth. He tried to think it out and to apply his scholarship as well as his candour to the question. His subsequent study of the Pentateuch got him into great trouble. He was deposed from his see, but was reinstated after an appeal to the Privy Council, only of course to be treated as outside the pale by his fellow dignitaries of the Church of England in South Africa. His situation was not quite as difficult as that of Galileo three centuries before. There must be few people now, even inside the two churches concerned, who would not say that Galileo's truth and Colenso's truth were the valid ones for the questions they raised, and that what they maintained was right.

The ordinary teacher is not a Galileo, nor even a Colenso. What ought he to do when such difficulties come his way? Rather nearer the present time, but still forty years ago, there was the famous trial in Dayton, Tennessee, of a biology teacher who taught the concept of Evolution, not as a theory in the sense of a mere surmise but in the sense of a generalisation from a great deal of evidence which in its broad lines was accepted as a ruling concept by biologists. It was in conflict with what people in the so-called Bible Belt believed to be true because the Book of Genesis said so. Both accounts, one of a special creation of separate species and the other of the gradual emergence of the species we know over a long period of evolutionary time, could not be true. Hardly anyone now would not agree that the teacher was wrongfully dismissed. But is that because we think he was right on the substance of the case? Suppose we agreed with the parents in the Bible Belt that the account in Genesis was literally true, would we still say that the teacher was right to tell his pupils that the majority if not virtually all biologists accepted the concept of evolution?

Surely there can be no doubt about the answer; and on two grounds. My first ground would be that of the principle classically enunciated by John Stuart Mill, that the only acceptable reply to a proposition advanced as true is a demonstration that it is not true, not an authoritarian veto on discussion. My other argument would be prudential, that in the long run it is impossible to isolate a culture with one belief system from the rest of the world, so that when your students discovered that you had been teaching them bad biology they would not thank you. This is not a matter of substituting one dogma for another. If the general concept of Evolution is over-turned (as in some respects Darwinism may have been modified) it will be because of new evidence, not because of what is said in the Bible. A scientist is only tentatively confident in his hypothesis. What he is really confident about is his method of finding things out. Within the realm of propositional statements as to what is, there is not room both for truth as so understood and a 'higher' truth that accommodates contradictions of truth as so under-stood. I can see no answer to the arguments brought forward in support of this view by Miss Kathleen Nott in her book *The Emperor's Clothes*.[3]

This is not to say that there may not be experiences more important to us that the recognition of information provided by the sciences. A profoundly felt, imaginative response to life, as in great tragedy, is more significant to many people, and much as I value the knowledge of man and his place in the universe given us by the sciences I would include myself among these. It is here, not in different accounts of factual evidence, that no contradic-tion lies. As I said earlier, I would not use the word 'truth' to describe the experience given us by a great tragedy any more than I would use it to describe the experience given us by great music. But if others do so use it they must make clear that they are not using the word in the correspondence sense and are not, through such a confusion, bemusing people into accept-ing what in the correspondence meaning of the term they would not accept.

We do understand what we mean when at the commonsense level of discourse we speak of facts. Equally we understand that we mean by truth our perception of external reality, a perception that, if necessary after dis-cussion and re-examination, we may expect others to share. It is said that the poet Blake, when asked where his visions occurred to him, pointed to his head. They were in there, not 'out there'. He knew the difference between the two levels of discourse. This is not to say that his visions were less real to him than his ordinary experiences, but they did not contradict these.

In education it is indispensible to initiate the young into both these worlds, the imaginative and the knowledge-based, and not to let them sup-pose that the function of one is to supersede what the other tells us is so or not so. In the realm that I have been concerned with here, nothing, it seems to me, should over-ride the principle that the great editor, C. P. Scott, enunciated for his newspaper: 'Opinions are free, but facts are sacred.'

This, as I see it, should be the relationship of beliefs to facts. The relation-ship of beliefs to values confronts us with, if anything, even more difficult problems. Normally we use the term 'values' to indicate those qualities that are of the greatest importance to us. But qualities of what? Of our-selves or of the things or situations we experience? Much ingenuity has gone into the discussion of this question, but I am going to leave it on one side. I agree with Stephen Toulmin who says, in his *The Place of Reason in Ethics*,[4] that it has distracted us from the really important question, which is whether the things we do value most are the things we ought to value most.

Now those things that we do value highly we often value so highly that we elevate respect for them to the status of a principle. Such principles have been closely associated with beliefs. It does not follow that the two are to be identified with each other, though loose thinkers have frequently done so. People who share common values may have different beliefs, for instance as to the origins of their values. A Christian and a Humanist might place honesty equally high in their scale of values, but the Christian would say that the source of his values was in a God, the Humanist that it was in our experience of man and society.

J. H. Barnsley in his book *The Social Reality of Ethics*[5] says that tolerance is a value put high in the Hindu religion and that it is closely related to the Hindu belief that there are many ways to God. It is almost a logical consequence of this. There is, I think, no doubt that some beliefs promote some values more than others. But the criteria for establishing the grounds for a belief and a value are not the same. When we ask for the grounds of a belief we refer to factual evidence, the nature of things. When we ask why it is good to insist on a certain value (especially if we wish to carry conviction to people outside our own belief system) we appeal less to immediate perceptions of external reality and more to reflections on human experience. Of course some statements may be ambiguous. What do we mean when we say that honesty is the best policy? It could mean that as a matter of fact those who are honest are the most successful, no doubt because people trust them. Or it could express a value judgement: that whether we succeed materially or not, it is right for a man to be honest. It turns on what is meant by best. In this example, the former meaning is probably that generally intended. To support it we should have to marshall the evidence. (It has been said that the Quakers tended to succeed in business because they were honest in their dealings; but a member of the Society of Friends would not say he was honest in business in order to succeed, but because he thought it right.) When we say that something is right we are not outside the possibilities of rational discussion, but we are perceptibly farther from the world of evidence.

There is more hope that others will agree with us in matters of fact than in moral or aesthetic evaluations. Facts do not vary so much with individual experience and are not as culture-bound as values. We can appeal to common experience and reflect upon it in discussing our values, but we cannot do this with the same degree of objectivity as with matters of fact. In the one case you can adduce your reasons. In the other you can appeal more directly to the evidence.

Although we use the term belief to describe convictions that are not completely demonstrable, nevertheless they involve in such large part decisions as to what is so that one might have supposed there would be more agreement in the world about them than there is. (Perhaps I should note that I am considering propositions of the form 'I believe *that* . . .'. Believing *in* merely means having special confidence in.) There are great differences in what people believe to be so, and they are strongly held. However, it remains true that, given a certain measure of tolerance, a society can still cohere though its members do have very different beliefs. What is certain is that there are some quite basic values without which there could not be a human society worthy of the name. That there are always a few people who do not recognise these does not alter that fact. The point is that they are exceptions and are so dealt with by the law or by opinion.

These basic values are, for instance, recognition of the rights and interests of other people, a reasonable willingness to follow rules that are for the common good, a sense of duty to the community, a general level of honesty and an expectation of truth-telling in daily intercourse, and so on. Without common subscription to these every man's hand would be against every man and there would not be a human society. Too great a difference of interests may lead to a break-up of a society, but in such a case it is the difference of interests rather than a difference of beliefs that is likely to prevent the accommodation that would permit the society to continue functioning. Unless, of course, the holding of the beliefs is co-present with a reasonable tolerance, the society will break up too. Given this, however, there is no reason why we should not live together though we have different beliefs as to the relationship of the earth to the sun, the existence of super-natural powers or their mode of operation, or the best kind of political and economic system. I would maintain that a society, and an education, are better if they do not dragoon and brainwash the young and the old into sharing a single set of beliefs in politics or religion, but enable them to develop responsible powers of personal decision about these things. This is because those who take such a view put the value of personal truth-seeking high, and the reasons for putting it high are two: that in the long run finding out and acting on the truth is what gives men their power to survive and to flourish in their environment, and that this alone is compatible with human dignity, with being fully human.

I have not said that any value, even truth-seeking and truth-telling, is an absolute value. I have said that I place this very high on the scale. We all know the dilemma of the doctor who has to decide whether to tell a patient that he is suffering from a probably fatal illness. There is also a real dilemma for the politician in certain circumstances. Was President Roosevelt right to go so far in reassuring the American people that they were not for the moment virtually defenceless when their fleet had been destroyed by the Japanese at Pearl Harbor; or Sir Stafford Cripps in the post-war years to tell the House of Commons that he had no intention of devaluing the pound when he must have so decided? If the American people had panicked at that moment the war could have been lost, especially had the Japanese invaded. Had Sir Stafford Cripps said he intended to devalue the pound in advance much financial damage might have been done. If we force ourselves to be honest about this we are driven to admit that there might be moments when telling the truth, or at least the full truth, is not the most important moral value. (There was a story about a fourth Wise Man who, when a soldier intent on killing all the firstborn asked if there was a baby inside, and the infant Jesus was, said 'No'. Was he right or wrong?) Yet this is so terribly dangerous an admission that we feel instinct-ively that only a man of the utmost moral scruple could safely admit it even to himself. It is, however, enough to make it clear to me that we cannot speak of absolute values. Indeed I am somewhat puzzled when people do speak of them. What do they mean?

We can have an idea of something that is itself and nothing else. In that sense I suppose we can imagine absolute Truth or Goodness or Beauty. But how this works out and whether it is anything but an entirely abstract idea of formal perfection I do not see. The word I would use would not be absolute but pure, as when we say that water is pure if it contains nothing but hydrogen and oxygen or when we speak of pure delight. To deny that values must be relative to one another, that none can be invoked without consideration of others, seems to me unrealistic, even perverse. I do not quite like saying that human values are on a scale. That suggests something too invariable, with precisely measurable distances between one value and another; and life is not like that. What makes this a doubtful metaphor and talk of absolute values unreal is that when values come into conflict with one another we have to make the best resolution of them we can in circumstances that are never exactly the same.

For instance, most of us would rank honesty higher than affability. Sociable persons make life more cheerful but we recognise that there are times when the need to be honest must over-ride this. Some people will draw the line in one place, some in another, and actual situations are always different. If people differ markedly in their general conduct we say that they seem to have different values. But there are no absolutes about it. Of course, since we cannot stop to work out every problem from nothing we establish general guidelines to give us first approximations as to what we should do. These we call our principles. But even telling the truth, as we have seen, is not an absolute principle, though it very nearly is.

The most satisfactory account of values I know is in Professor W. H. Werkmeister's *Man and his Values*.[6] He says that we exist in a world that, for us, is as we perceive it, and to which we respond in terms of our nature. Our understanding may be faulty and our ability to change things narrowly limited, but it is in such situations that man forms his values. For each of us our perception of life begins with our own experience, and from the beginning we put greater value on some things than on others. We are born with exploratory drives, and at the same time live within limitations. We move towards what satisfies our drives without creating frustration through the too severe operation of these limitations. We are born into societies in which other men and women have had such experience before us and have, so to speak, objected what they have found to be their values. This, too, sets up tensions between our drives and the possibility of satisfying them without frustration. Each of us gradually establishes his own set of values, aiming at a balance between what his experience tells him he values and the need for adjustment to the limitations of human life, physical and social. These values can be reflected on and reasoned about. The great question is whether what we value most is what we ought to value most.

This seems to me the sense of the matter. There is great room for discussion as to how far the values we hold and act on are justified or not. But

I am not sure that there is a further level of discourse that would be profitable, especially if it is of the kind that tries to make moral philosophy a nostalgic substitute for a lost theology (God now equalling Absolute Values). That only tends to deflect us from what seems to be the essential soundness of the position I have described.

So far, although here and there I have indicated the bearing of the argument on education, I have considered facts, beliefs and values in general. I have argued that there is what we may call a commonsense level of discourse, based on the ordinary use of language, at which we may consider these questions and not feel altogether out of court although we may not be professional philosophers. I would now like to look briefly at the ways in which these general considerations apply to education and especially to teachers, most of whom are unlikely to have had specialist training as philosophers and yet must consider these questions because of their bearing on their work. What are the obligations of teachers to facts, beliefs and values, and what are they to do when they seem to conflict? First let us consider our obligations to facts.

The amount of factual information we are expected to pass on from one generation to another grows frightening. Yet we know that education is not merely a matter of passing on information. As has often been said, the merely well-informed man can be an awful bore. We scorn Mr Gradgrind and his 'Facts, facts, facts! ' but we have only recently realised that we ourselves in our teaching and our examinations have been overemphasising factual content. We could react too far. Without adequate knowledge no one can be an educated man. Inert facts are as dull as inert ideas. But information needs often to be full and can be interesting and illuminating. Not least, teaching a scrupulous regard for facts constitutes part of teaching regard for truth. Somehow we have got to find a new balance among these conflicting ideals.

Some adults never learn to distinguish fact from fantasy in a mature way; and all of us find that some truths are difficult to face. An indispensable function of education is to help us to do this better, and with more courage when the facts do not please us. We have to learn that arguments for a propositional statement must be tested by the evidence and reasonable deduction from it, not by what we might wish to believe. Facts are apt to be neutral to our desires, yet the understanding of ourselves and our environment rests on our ability to get at the real facts, knowing that we cannot have final certainty but not refusing acceptance when we have tested them as best we can.

The most familiar test of the teacher's equivalent of the Hippocratic Oath concerns his willingness to acknowledge his ignorance when he just does not know. The standard answer is the right one: that the risk to his authority if he says he does not know is less dangerous than the loss to his integrity if he tries to bluff. A friend of mine, inspecting a West African class which for some reason was on the unlikely subject of seals, was surprised to hear the teacher say, when asked what seals lived on, 'Bananas'. After the lesson he asked the teacher if he really thought the staple diet of seals was bananas. The teacher said he didn't know what their main food was, but had had to give some answer if he was not to lose his authority with the class. I suspect it did not take long for some bright boy to find him out in any case. But what was the teacher doing to himself? Education is not all about facts, but when facts are involved we must be honest about them.

This sounds easy: just see whether something is so or not, and report accordingly. Unfortunately it is more complicated. We do not just see that something is a fact. So far from just seeing, we have to observe. This is not quite the same, and it needs training. For we tend to see what we expect to see. Any proof-reader will tell you that if you follow what you know must be the sense you will miss the printing errors, for they should not be there and you assume that they are not. Doctors who have a strong intuition that they know what is wrong with a patient can miss a symptom that is under their eyes. So in teaching it is not only necessary to insist on respect for the facts but to train in exact, assumption-free observation. Among other things, an educated man is one who does not let his preconceptions dictate his perceptions. That in the larger sense is what fidelity to the facts means.

We often have to make up our minds without all the relevant facts. We have to decide how to act, even though the evidence is incomplete. We get all the evidence we can, try to evaluate it and realise that we are still farther from certainty than we might be in the abstracted situation of the laboratory. One of the uses of the study of history is that it shows the inevitability of this and gives us some training in nevertheless deciding when in imagination we put ourselves in such situations in the past with the benefit of hindsight.

Teaching that does not bring out the significance of facts is dull. No doubt it is wrong to read into facts what the evidence will not bear. Yet the bright boy or girl is the one who seizes on the facts that are significant (if only in the style of Robinson Crusoe and the footprint) and the genius is the man who can bring hitherto disparate facts within a single concept or formula. The jump may prove to be wrong when checked, as it must be. But it is better to encourage the imaginative leap than to let students remain fact-bound.

If we teach respect for facts but yet encourage the understanding of significance, how great is the danger that factual matter will kill the life of the imagination? That was what was worrying Keats when he wrote *Lamia*. The young man Lycius was in love with a woman who was evil, a lamia or serpent in disguise. But she was beautiful. His tutor, Apollonius, saw through her and with his stern regard for truth tried to save Lycius. All Lycius knew was that he was destroying beauty. 'Philosophy will clip an angel's wings.' 'There was an awful rainbow once in heaven,' but all we have now is the scientist's spectrum. This is one side of the argument. Keats in the poem leaves the question unresolved, for he did not want to force himself to a conclusion before he was ready to accept it. Had he lived I think he would have achieved a mature synthesis. He often insisted, for all his love of beauty, that he must make his poetry more 'philosophical'.

Of course scientific developments may affect the availability of symbols. People ask if the moon can ever be the same again now men have trodden on its surface. Not quite the same, perhaps, as a symbol of the unattainably lovely. On the other hand explorations of space are bringing new images – the earth as a spaceship to quote one that has already become a little trite. On the face of it there is no reason why a recognition of facts and an imaginative response to life should get in each other's way. It does not follow that a man who understands that speech functions are located in a special part of the brain is thereby made contemptuous of poetry or that someone who knows the body to be 70 per cent water is thereby contemptuous of man's creative powers.

If insistence on facts is crude it can go with a repression of the imaginative powers. That was Gradgrind's fault. Dickens was not being very extravagant in his picture of the grim utilitarian, as the example of John Stuart Mill's education reminds us.

This does raise questions about the balance of studies. Is there too little scope, especially in the education of boys, for the arts of expression? The balance we strike depends on the qualities we think important in living. In his speech to the Sixth Commonwealth Education Conference, Mr Manley, the prime minister of Jamaica, said that of the five main things he would want a school to do even in a country of scant resources, one was that 'it must be involved with every form of creative activity. This is to ensure that children grow up to see cultural activities as an opportunity for self-expression as much as a process by which one is inspired and entertained through the efforts of others.' How like a West Indian to insist on this! Later the delegates were taken to a splendid evening of Jamaican singing and dancing. And who was the leading male dancer? The head of the extra-mural department of the university. Now I admit that our culture is not the same as that of the West Indies. Perhaps it would not be felt appropriate for the vice-chancellor of Oxford to go dancing down the High, or for the principal of the Canberra College of Advanced Education to lead a ballet on what there passes for a lawn. But with due adaptation to our different ways, would it not be good if something of the sort could happen?

It may be rather a jump from more or less philosophic talk about facts and values to speculations of this diverting kind. But in reality it isn't. What a community makes of its life depends on what it thinks good. Do we think music, dancing, poetry, drama to be as important a part of life as the facts and skills we need to control our environment and to qualify us for a career?

A school will in general reflect the values of the society or the group in society that sponsors it. As a community itself it must stand for the basic values without which no community can cohere. But this is not a matter of automatic reflection. Even the most hard-pressed school has some scope for setting standards itself and for promoting thought in the young about their values. When it comes to personal values it is perhaps more important that a teacher should convey that he has considered values than that he should continuously insist on the values that he has. The values of his students may be different but they will respect the fact that a teacher has his standards.

I agree with Mr Patrick Souper, whose forthcoming book *About to Teach*[7] I have had the pleasure of reading in typescript, that a good teacher is so more by what he is than by what in any formal sense he does. He will have disappointments and frustrations, quite inevitably, and he will only be able to support these and make them part of a good total experience if inside him he has a well-considered assurance of personal values and beliefs.

But if he should not insist too overtly on his purely personal values (as distinct from those without which a society cannot cohere) this is an even more necessary caution in the matter of beliefs, at any rate in a school in a public system. He should, I think, be ready to state them when invited, especially in the higher forms of a school. But in a society like ours he is bound to have in his classes representation of more than one system of beliefs. He, certainly, has his own; but he has been entrusted by the whole multi-belief society with the education of its children, and this is a position that he should not abuse. Two things he can and should do. The first is to show that serious questions, including the political and the religious, should be taken seriously. He should not discourage discussion of them, but with himself as chairman rather than protagonist inside the school. (Outside he should be free.) And the second thing he should do is to teach the necessity of tolerance. He should explain the difference between tolerance of persons and their right to their views, and on the other hand the bland assumption that all views are equally good (which of course no one who takes such questions seriously can believe).[8]

Only people so confident of their own belief systems that they shut their minds to evidence and people so lacking in respect for others that they are repressively intolerant will want to bring up a new generation in blinkers. This is a denial of the very postulates of education, which must be to develop responsible, critical minds. Not every question can be left without a provisional answer with children of every age, but it is one thing to pass on beliefs grounded in knowledge that is publicly verifiable and another thing to refuse to consider whether this is so.

It may be said that these things I have been saying are the facile aspirations of a liberal idealist. I do not think so. They are rather the basic principles of a good education and a good society. I do not mind even using the word 'good'. We are sometimes hesitant to use the word for fear of conjuring up a picture of the repressive authoritarians of the past. But the aim of a good school will be to help children and young people to develop into good persons. That is what we want and what their parents want. And what is more, it is what we should want.

We shall only be able to play our part in this within a well thought-out framework of ideas about facts and beliefs and values. What moral and analytical philosophers have written on these things is important, but a great deal of what ought to be said can be said at the level of hard-thinking yet sensitive commonsense. If that is so, what I have said in this chapter, so far from being an exercise in abstractions, may involve (as I think it does) some of the most important things in education and in the preparation of teachers for their work.

Chapter 6

Can We Work Together
If Our Beliefs Differ?

The question with which I have headed this chapter looks like a practical one. In some measure, of course, it is. But I have put it in this section of this book because the answer is going to be determined very largely by our attitudes to those from whom we differ in beliefs, and our attitudes depend very largely on our understanding the difference between two concepts, beliefs and values. As I said in the last chapter, these two things are commonly associated; but they are by no means identical. We often share important values with people from whom we differ in beliefs, whether they be religious or political. It seems to me that where we do share values it is normally possible to work well in education with those with whom we differ in beliefs, but that where important values differ then it is much more difficult. This is the question I would like to take up in this chapter.

Let me first point out how important the question is. In any national society now there must be a public system of education. In countries like our own we nevertheless agree that if special communities, normally but not always religious ones, wish to set up their own schools they have the right to do so. But this does not solve the problem of collaboration between groups with sharply differing systems of belief. For one thing, only the larger of such groups, if they are not satisfied with the public provision, will have the resources in people and funds to establish schools of their own. The problem of collaboration among the groups that stay in the public system will remain. Secondly, the public system and any private one will have to relate to one another in many ways. The private system will ask for financial help from the state, and with this must go some arrangement to satisfy the government that conditions, physical and educational, satisfy reasonable requirements. The examinations taken in the schools are likely to be identical, for all sorts of cogent practical reasons. Therefore there is bound to be some joint consultation about curricula and syllabuses, however much freedom is recognised as allowable. Thirdly, and most important, if the posture in public is always one of mutual confrontation and never of joint consultation about common professional problems, the country as well as education will suffer.

There are countries where no private school is allowed and all the public schools have to inculcate the official ideology. This is true of communist countries. There are others where a particular religion is so dominant that for practical purposes there are hardly any private schools owing allegiance to some other view of life. This is true of some Moslem countries and of Roman Catholic Spain. This, however, does not solve their problem. They still have to face it internationally. This is true both at the inter-governmental level, in an organisation like Unesco, and at the professional level, in the arrangements for the meeting and interchange of experience between teachers, scholars and research workers of different countries. What ideas do we bring to such meeting for collaboration, either within countries or internationally? And what bearing have they on our practice?

Most religious belief-systems, and some political ones, claim to be comprehensive. That is to say, if you are a good Catholic or a good Communist this should influence, one might almost say govern, everything in your private and your public life. Such powerful and comprehensive belief-systems naturally want education to be firmly in their control. They would really prefer there not to be any education system that had an ideology different from their own, for they, and they alone, have the truth. This does not predispose their adherents to think that there is much scope for collaboration in education with those who hold different beliefs. The distinction between beliefs and values would not impress them: they claim that their system covers both, and that although there may be shared values in a sense (honest men, for instance, outside their own group) the beliefs are so essential for reinforcing the values that the values cannot be relied on without them. It is possible to retain this view and make it effective within an area over which the dominant ideology has complete control.

Life on this globe now, however, is less and less permissive of complete isolation. In such regimes or parties those who travel or have even official intercourse with people of other beliefs begin to acquire at least a surface tolerance; and with many it goes beneath the mere surface. They discover that there are at least professional interests in common. They learn at least a code for working together up to a point. They have to. And the question that I have put at the head of this chapter then inevitably begins to enter into their minds.

These are the adherents of firm and often intolerant orthodoxies. The question is no less serious for the person who considers himself liberal and more tolerant. How far can he hope to work in education with people who hold their beliefs much more dogmatically than he does? He may be just as determined a fighter against rigid belief-systems as they are in their defence. Can he act as if their adherence to rigid belief-systems does not affect his collaboration with them? May a liberal-minded person not feel (as one visitor to the Soviet Union said on returning to England) that they are so intolerant of critical ideas that they don't know what education is about? If the people you are expected to work with know they have the truth and the whole truth, how far can you hope to persuade yourself that you share educational values with them? Let us have the surface courtesies in international meetings, by all means; but let us not delude ourselves, it may be said, into supposing that there is anything more than that.

Perhaps it is easier to look at this sort of problem first within national

societies where there is something like a common outlook even though
there are great divergencies of belief. We can start with England itself.

I had first to try to think this question out nearly thirty years ago and
was prompted to write an article about it.[1] Times have changed but I
would like to revert to the argument I tried to counter then and the reasons
I gave for thinking that we could have a coherent educational policy, even
though in this country there were great differences of view in both politics
and religion and in what then were still called philosophies of life.

This all started with a discussion rather pushed by the *Times Educational Supplement*. It had quoted a publication called the *Christian News
Letter* as saying that although it would be wrong for Christians to impose
their views by authority on people who did not share them, nevertheless we
could not have a coherent educational policy because we were divided in
our ultimate beliefs. The TES summed the matter up in a leading article[2]
by saying: 'What is the nature of man; that he is merely human, or also
divine? Until an answer to that question is given there can be no certain
ends in education, nor any philosophy.' The word 'philosophy', incidentally, looked a little odd even then as it was used in that discussion. It would
look even odder now. Those who used it seemed to mean something like
'outlook' and clearly sighed for a universal Christian outlook. In other
words it was a polite way of saying 'religion', which really wouldn't do.

Perhaps I might quote one paragraph in which, after saying that it was
vain to hope for such widespread agreement in our society on ultimate
beliefs, I argued that my own experience, and indeed increasingly that of
our society, did not warrant such pessimism. If we could not all agree in
beliefs, we could often agree on the values that were important. I wrote:

> It is easy when discussing ultimate beliefs to persuade oneself into a
> conviction of exclusive merit, but what is our actual experience of work-
> ing in education with those who differ from us in these matters? Is it not,
> that given only one thing (the same freedom to express our thoughts
> that we concede to others) we find over and over again that we have a
> large measure of agreement with colleagues who would differ from us
> if we started discussing philosophy or religion? And agreement not
> merely as to means, but as to values? Speaking only for myself I must
> say that outside such direct questions as to whether a particular doctrine
> should be officially taught in educational establishments I have found no
> such paralysing difference as apparently I ought. I am forced to ask
> myself whether this indicates philosophical naïveté on my part or
> whether it represents something real on which, in a tolerant but diverse-
> minded democracy, we can really build. Is the experience of a non-
> sectarian body like the Workers' Educational Association (where we
> certainly seem to share important and activating values) merely a transi-
> tional illusion? Is the fact that freethinkers could work so happily with a
> President who was later to become the Archbishop of Canterbury merely
> an indication either that they were really Christians or that he was not?
> What is the experience of our universities since the abolition of religious

tests? Do divisions on educational policy there really follow credal lines? I don't think this is anyone's experience, except where a quite specifically religious question is raised. It simply doesn't occur to anyone to look for divisions of opinion about university education among students, faculty members or governing bodies, in such terms. Our best allies in matters that concern our sense of educational values are often those from whom we should have to divide if these questions were brought in.

But what are these educational values on which, in this country, most of us can agree? I suggested that although there were many dispositions we would wish education to foster, everyone would agree that an education was a poor one that did not foster three things in particular: intellectual honesty, imaginative vitality and a sense of right and wrong. One of the great difficulties has been to adjust the imaginative and the moral life to the great social and scientific changes that have taken place, and this has meant that some things on which previous generations would have taken their stand are now either not believed at all or are believed in a more relative and less absolute way. It is this difficult process of readjustment that has produced so much confusion in our educational philosophy; but insofar as we do suffer from confusion this is at least very closely allied to the intellectual vitality and development without which we might as well be dead. A country is wise to base its education on the best values in its own experience. No country has learned so clearly from its own experience the wisdom of trying to co-operate on the level of action, irrespective of disagreement about ultimates, or has with such marked success developed the friendly techniques for carrying the ideal into practice. This is the essential thing in our not so incoherent philosophy of educational practice. It would surely be wise to understand this, to cherish it and to continue to do so in the changing circumstances of our times.

If I felt that then, I feel it even more strongly now. But the passage of nearly thirty years does prompt two comments. Can one be so confident as I was then that we indeed have this sense of shared values? And could the tradition of which I spoke go by default under the pressures from which our society now suffers?

When I said, a few years ago, that there were general values to which we could appeal in English society when seeking a consensus about moral education, even though of course there were differences about particular courses of action, a master from my own old school wrote to me to say that there no doubt used to be but he did not think there now were. You could not appeal in terms of general principles like fair play, regard for others, telling the truth, and so on, as once you could. I was disquieted by this letter.

It is extremely difficult to draw up a balance sheet in such a matter between one period and another. There was far less security for the ordinary person in the daily life of Elizabethan England than now. Their sturdy rogues and vagabonds were much more of a menace than our football hooligans and muggers. Standards of honour in political life were much lower than they are now. It is difficult for us even to feel our minds into the conduct of a really great man like Bacon, to say nothing of Sir Walter Raleigh. Virtù was so different from virtue. Yet no one can read the plays of Shakespeare without feeling that there were standards of good and bad, right and wrong, honour and dishonour, that were not merely his private standards but that he knew that he and his public shared. Again, in the eighteenth century there was violence, both outside the law and within its provisions, that still shocks us. It was dangerous to walk the streets of London at night; and if you did you certainly carried a stout stick. Corruption in public life was shameless. Yet a moralist like Dr Johnson knew there were standards on which in a large measure he could rely in speaking to his fellow countrymen.

The second half of the nineteenth century in England was a period in which tolerance was largely extended, corruption in public life was very nearly eliminated and the cities and the roads were made safe for ordinary people going about their affairs. But this is not the whole story. Life was very different for the 'submerged tenth'. Fagin and his gang were not mere inventions of melodrama. Leonard Woolf in his autobiography tells how middle-class and professional families were conscious that outside their milieu there was the mob, not the working class as a whole but the *lumpenproletariat*.[3] They were afraid of them and looked to the policeman for their protection. They also tried, through philanthropic work, to spread middle-class values, some of which reflected their own propertied privilege but many of which were necessary in any reputable society. (Bernard Shaw could let his dustman laugh at this middle-class morality precisely because there was little real danger.) Not least, these values were transmitted through the elementary schools, and after the turn of the century through the new secondary schools. The independent schools prepared their young to be officers in this society, the elementary schools prepared the privates, the secondary schools the NCOs; but the moral values they inculcated were substantially the same. This framework has been badly shaken in the period of increasing violence that the world has gone through since 1914, and the fact that this country has not been torn by invasion and by civil strife has not saved us from many of the side-effects.

It is not altogether easy to distinguish between what ought to have gone and what ought not. On the whole the shift in power and influence as between social groups has been right; but the greater readiness to resort to violence, the falling-off in standards of personal honesty, the lack of consideration for the well-being of society as a whole compared with the short-term advantage of the individual or the group, have been wrong. It may well be that there are large sections of the school population, reflecting large sections of the adult population, to which appeals in terms of social values will produce only a hoarse laugh – and emphatically not only in the working-class population, if that term means anything any more. The schools cannot put all this right by themselves; but if there is a section in the school population that no longer responds when an appeal is made to those values without which there cannot be any good society, of any political description, that is a measure of the need to make moral preparation for adult life a much more serious thing than it has been in these last decades. Basically I think the values are still there. But with a proportion of young people, as of adults, we have neglected the educationally primary task of leading them to see that if they ignore others then others will ignore them; and that way chaos and general misery lie.

The second question, whether our on the whole good traditions in tolerance and collective concern could go by the board under the pressures of the times, is related to the first. Clearly they could. The more we realise that, the less likely it is that they will. The forces of cohesion are in fact very strong in English society, in spite of the constant pressures of sectional interest. We are still in much better social state than some of the other countries of Europe and our traditional skills in accommodating rival interests fairly and without violence are by no means exhausted. What matters is that we should realise how many values we do have in common, however much we differ in religious or political beliefs.

This is not so easily said when one looks at the international educational scene. In the early days of Unesco the ex-enemy totalitarian countries, Germany and Japan, were not members; nor was the Soviet Union; nor was Franco's Spain. There was a broad consensus of values: they were those of the Western liberal tradition. When in turn the Soviet Union and Spain applied for membership a decision of principle had to be taken. Was Unesco to be a club of like-minded members or a forum where all countries, whatever their kind of regime, should take part? The admittance of the Soviet Union and Spain meant a decision for the latter proposition, as indeed in the United Nations itself. There can be very little doubt that this was right. Once you begin subjecting governments to some kind of ideological test then rather few are likely to remain members, and the advantages of a universal forum go. Nevertheless the difficulties of formulating common aims in terms of values were enhanced and the opportunity to play politics with the organisation was enhanced too.

The differences in educational values between, for example, the schools and universities of the Soviet Union and our own are too great to be ignored. For them the insistence on Marxist ideology as interpreted by the Communist Party over-rules everything else. Anything like an organised campaign of criticism of orthodoxy is repressed. Views in scientific matters can gain massive official support if they square, or seem to square, with orthodoxy, even though scientists elsewhere, and (till they are silenced) in the Soviet Union, repudiate them (the views of the biologist Lysenko are a case in point). Yet in this country not even the Communist Party has been declared illegal. There are Communist dons and Communist headmasters, and if there are so few of them that cannot be because they have been refused opportunity for expressing their views. The critical intelligence that asks questions that are awkward for orthodoxy is here a value in itself. How then can representatives of these two sets of values work together in any meaningful way?

The first way in which they can work together is technical. Ideological questions are not likely to come up in a meeting among those who are devising ways and means of bringing water to arid lands, or of those who are perfecting the means for detecting likely earthquakes in advance. One can go much further than this: in areas where social and governmental questions may arise, such as the ways in which illiteracy may be eradicated, there is a large technical area where the exchange of experience may be interesting and useful to all concerned.

Such discussion, and frequently collaboration, starts the habit of relationship. If a point comes up that involves different values it has to be clarified and each position argued, not given domination by force. At first this may affect only the few who participate, and they, if they come from a totalitarian regime, are likely to be well-grounded in the faith, to be not easily open to defection. So one must not exaggerate the effect. The same is true of collaboration in an international secretariat. It has long been believed by non-Communist members of the Unesco secretariat that there has always been a Communist cell therein. This is in flagrant contradiction to the affirmation members of the secretariat make to serve the international community impartially while they are members. But it would be difficult to point to any successful plot to turn policy this way or that. It was the Americans, during the McCarthy era, who did more than the Russians ever did to demand publicly that international civil servants who were their nationals should be subject to a surveillance by Unesco that was to serve their national government's ends, not those of the international community. But in spite of such difficulties, and the need sometimes to let sleeping dogs lie, something does happen from the sheer habit of working together among people from different kinds of regime.

Why should this be so? Because there still are values, whatever our differences of creed, that are human and to which appeal can be made. These may be stirred to save Venice from sinking in the waters or ancient Egyptian monuments from being covered by waters that man has raised through a dam; or it may be through collaboration in a mixed team advising an educationally ill-developed country how to expand and improve its education.

Whether this adds up to much or little, a start in building a world consciousness in education has got to be made, as part of the movement to world order without which civilisation will sooner or later collapse. We have to emerge into the human, transcending our divisions for those purposes for which that is necessary. That can only be based on common human values. These will not be all our values. But it is much more likely that we shall achieve a sense of sharing the important ones with all human beings than that we shall all agree in matters of belief, religious or political. That is why, it seems to me, it is very important indeed to hold clear in our minds the distinction between these two concepts.

Chapter 7

The Concept of Rights in Education

There are certain key concepts in educational thought that have been the subject of analysis and inquiry not only by philosophers but by historians, moralists and social scientists. In this chapter and the next I would like to take two of these concepts and ask whether, although necessarily drawing on what the specialists have said, we can apply commonsense to understand them better. These two concepts are those of Rights and of Equality. I shall consider them first in general and then in special relation to education, and I begin with Rights.

On the plinth of the statue of Danton in the Latin Quarter of Paris one can read the words, 'Après le pain, le plus grand besoin du peuple est l'éducation'. This sounds a new note in human history. It is true that the kings of Prussia had had the idea of universal elementary education, but less because of the assertion of the people's need than because they themselves needed it to give their people a corporate sense and bring them within the apparatus of the State. It is also true that Danton's words expressed simply an aspiration, one that took nearly a century to translate into reality. But the need had been felt, and eloquently expressed.

From the sense of a need to the assertion of a right the step can be a short one. Professor Raphael points out[1] that the right to education is included in the second Declaration of the Rights of Man and the Citizen, in 1793. It is also to be found in the Second Part of Tom Paine's *Rights of Man* of the year before. What is at first sight surprising is that Burke speaks of the 'right to instruction' in his *Reflections on the French Revolution* of 1790,[2] for Burke is known as the enemy of the idea of natural rights. Burke never set out systematically his conception of rights, but he did distinguish between rights that were supposed to inhere in man in a state of nature and his real rights, those that derived from the civil society in which he lived. The idea was clearly very much in the air.

We are speaking, of course, of countries of Western civilisation. It is only in our time that education has been recognised as a universal human right, and I think that future historians will note that as one of the remarkable things about our present century. It was the Declaration of Human Rights adopted by the United Nations in 1948 that said, 'Education is a universal human right'. Then why, the innocent may ask, do we not have it throughout the world? Alas, anyone who has to turn a general principle into a law, or a law into administrative reality, has many problems in his way; and some of these do not occur to those who make the resounding declarations. Some of these problems are practical, and especially financial. Some, however, are conceptual.

If anyone should think that this is a matter of theory with little bearing on practice I would invite him to keep his eye on the press for a few days and note how often the claim to something as a right occurs, and then observe how rarely the claimants appear to have thought out what they mean by a right and to have examined the relationship between the right they claim and the other rights that others claim.*

There are rights of different kinds, some concerned with civil freedoms, some with social welfare. There are claims of different orders of intensity, some very basic, others advanced only in relation to a given state of development. The question that arises is whether any right can be considered to be absolute or whether we must regard them as relative, relative to each other (as when two rights seem to conflict) and relative to circumstances and practical possibilities. This is recognised in effect in Article 26 of the Universal Declaration, which claims elementary education as a universal right but says of technical and professional education only that it should be accessible generally and of higher education that it should be accessible on the basis of merit.

Other current uses of the word raise yet more questions. Have students a right to free tuition and adequate maintenance irrespective of the income of their parents? What is the relation of rights to duties? Is it reasonable to say that grants are given for study and that if a student neglects his studies or tries to disrupt a college or university then he has morally forfeited any right he may have had to his grant?

Again, pupils may be said to have rights; but are they not modified by their status as pupils? There is a real sense in which children have rights. But have they a right (as it has been claimed in some quarters) to choose their own school, and even the adults with whom they live their domestic lives? The general community has its rights – a point sometimes forgotten by the eager defenders of the rights of a section of a community. (I once heard Mr Herbert Morrison say, after he had been deluged with protests at

---

* To analyse the confusions in particular examples would take space and time. My purpose at the moment is simply to note the frequency with which claims occur without any serious attempt at justification. As I was making the first draft of this chapter I noted an interview given by Mrs Thatcher (then minister of education) to the *Sunday Times* (8 April 1973) in which she invoked the right of parents to choose their children's school, and for which I don't think she would have got a very high mark had she read politics instead of chemistry at Oxford. I noticed a hostile leading article in the *Daily Telegraph* on the Russell Report (Adult Education) which guyed its recommendations with ironic echoes of the 'inalienable rights' of the American Declaration of Independence. On the same day I received an appeal about the education of the children of the Palestinian refugees, a matter with which I had been much concerned in the education department of Unesco. This said that education was the right of every child and the life-line of these refugees, clearly a different order of claim from either of the previous two. Pretty well any week would yield similar examples.

a Labour Party Conference about the rights of minorities, that majorities had rights too.)

I hope that the examples I have given will have shown that we must be clear about what we mean by a right if there are not to be confusing consequences for policy and practice, and that getting clear about it is something that demands careful thought and cannot be settled by mere rhetoric. To these conceptual difficulties I should like to turn now.

The three initial points I want to make are: first, that rights are not inherent in a man's nature as a human being but are accorded by the society in which he lives; secondly, that they are not absolute but must be considered in relation to other rights; and thirdly, that because they are social and relative, rights should be seen as emergent and associated with the practicability of recognising them in any given state of development. Then I would like to consider the relation of rights to duties. After that I think we can approach the grand question: what are the kinds of ground we can properly give to justify the recognition of some particular claim as a right? These, it will be noted, are general questions about the nature of rights. It is essential that we understand what we mean by rights in general before we can profitably discuss rights in education. But because it is rights in education that are our immediate concern I shall draw most of my examples from that field of debate.

Man is biologically a social animal, that is his 'nature'. The idea of a state of nature before man lived in societies is not only unhistorical but unhelpful as a metaphor, for if man is by nature social then a state of nature is unnatural. It has been said before that if a man were in reality alone on a desert island as long as Robinson Crusoe he would by the end of the time almost certainly have lost his human faculties, and these Crusoe had only because he had lived with other men before he was cast away. What is certain is that no question of rights arose while he was alone on the island. Even his right to possess it could only have arisen when someone else came along to challenge him for it. The reader begins to wonder about rights only when Man Friday joins Crusoe: he may speculate as to Crusoe's rights over Friday and as to Friday's rights in relation to Crusoe. If all this is so obvious, does it dispose of the matter? A feeling haunts me that it does not, for the immense number of writers and speakers who have invoked this concept surely cannot all have been under the spell of a metaphor that was empty. Even today the idea of natural rights lingers on. It is in the first Article of the Declaration of 1948: 'All human beings are born free and equal in dignity and rights.' This is an odd statement, for the very reason for the Declaration was precisely that they are not. The rum Rousseau-istic ring of this first statement is enough to make Edmund Burke turn in his grave.

There are, I think, two explanations of the peculiar hold of this concept of 'natural' rights. One is historical, explaining what the users of this phrase in the eighteenth century really had in mind by it. The other turns on a special, though by no means unprecedented, sense of the word 'nature' and is of continuing significance today if we are to understand the moral force that we so often feel behind claims for the recognition of rights.

Margaret Macdonald in a paper on 'Natural rights'[3] points out that the attempt to argue that there are rights because reason shows them to inhere in human nature breaks down, first because a state of nature never existed, and secondly because the differing lists of such supposed rights from Hobbes to Maritain show there is no clear 'nature' from which they can be deduced. Yet the idea persists, and this is because it expresses the values that are felt to be necessary for any human society. She sees the declaration that something is a right not as the assertion of a proposition but as a declaration as to which side you are on when there is controversy about what kind of a society there should be. Reading this back into the controversies of the eighteenth century one might say that those who attacked the *ancien régime* as a bad kind of society appealed to 'nature' in the sense that it was not man in himself who was wrong but a bad society that made him wrong. It ignored his rights, as well as corrupting him in many ways. This is as much as to say that if we had a society that would let men's nature develop as it could and might, instead of one that denied his potentialities and ignored his rights, life would be happier and better for us.

Now this is not too far from the sense of the word 'nature' which has in mind not just what an animal or a man may be at a particular stage of development, but the potentialities already in him (part, therefore, of his nature) for developing further. A right, seen in this light, is the recognition of a claim that he should have this or that (education, for instance) because without it his nature cannot flower as it should. When people realise that they are being cut off from a kind of life of which, if the rights were acknowledged, they would be fully capable, then a sense of a moral wrong is engendered. There is tremendous moral force behind the claims men make that their rights should be recognised, and this is surely its source. The spokesmen for 'natural rights' got it wrong, in that historically there was never a state of nature, and in that rights are conferred by a society instead of inhering in the nature of men as individuals; but although they used the wrong rationalisations I believe they had grasped the essential point, which my gloss on their theories has tried to bring out. And this surely explains why the concept of natural rights has held such sway and even now is not quite abandoned.

In the plea for education as a right it is the moral force of it that comes over so strongly. When Jude the Obscure wrote on the walls of the Oxford college 'I have understanding as well as you', he was making a bitter moral protest against his exclusion. When the refugees from Palestine in their first miserable camps demanded education for their children even if their rations had to be cut, they were making a claim to a moral entitlement. Education may be said to be a 'welfare right' rather than a basic civil right; but the moral force behind the claim, and the underlying reasoning, are the same.

The anti-slavery movement has been essentially a moral protest. Slavery was seen as an offence against human nature. Professor Hart[4] regards the right to be free as perhaps the one 'natural' right, using that word in its old sense. Take it in its simplest form as referring to legal status: it is an offence against any man's natural rights that he should be born into slavery. But what does this mean? It means that without the legal status of free men people cannot realise their nature as human. If they are slaves they are not human beings, they are living tools. One can make this statement without invoking some imagined state of nature before civil society began. Indeed the reference is precisely to what a civil society prescribes.

What is the basis of the movement for equal rights for women? Surely the same. To hold them in subjection is to deny them the possibility of realising their humanity as they otherwise could.

There may be differences of priority between such fundamental civil and legal claims, but they are all social, claims as to how people should be treated in a just society. They are more fundamental, if you like, than claims for 'welfare rights', like education, just as the claims for the education of the young are more fundamental than the claims for the further education of adults, as the Russell Report recognised. But the basis for the claim that education should be recognised as a right is the same: that without this, human beings cannot be as fully and richly human as they otherwise could be.

Professor Morris Ginsberg[5] traced the extension of the concept of rights from groups of people to man universally, and from law and politics to welfare, and he emphasised the moral significance of these changes:

> These movements point, I think, to a valuable element in the theory of natural rights, namely the subordination of politics to ethics. On this view there are moral rights and duties, wherever there is human intercourse, though there may be no durable 'societies' and no States, that is to say politically organised societies. In this sense there are rights of man as such. There are *recognised* rights wherever there are societies with a regular structure, though there may be no differentiated machinery for promulgation and enforcement. There are *legal* rights in societies that have a developed judiciary and organs of enforcement. The legal rights may or may not be in harmony with recognised moral rights or with moral rights not widely recognised but demonstrably justifiable as conditions or constituents of well-being.

It is as soon as law concerns itself on a serious scale with welfare as well as with civil organisation that the question of welfare rights becomes serious.

That we may legitimately speak of human welfare rights as well as of political rights is widely accepted. Professor Cranston, however, calls this in question in his admirably lucid book, *What are Human Rights?*[6] He notes that the traditional human rights are political and civil rights such as the right to life, liberty and a fair trial. What are now being put forward as universal human rights are economic and social rights, such as the right to unemployment insurance, old-age pensions, medical services and holidays with pay. He says that philosophically this does not make sense and that politically the confusion it causes hinders the protection of what are correctly seen as human rights. (A little earlier Professor Cranston describes welfare rights as of a different logical category, being specific, not human in the sense of pertaining to all men. I think I am right in assuming that he does not deny that there may be such rights, but he criticises their inclusion in declarations and covenants of *universal* human rights.)

No doubt we can conveniently distinguish between civic and welfare rights, but if there are rights of both kinds we must look for some other distinguishing criterion if we criticise their inclusion in common charters. (That Communist countries have ridden away on claims that their record in welfare rights is good, although they deny civic rights such as freedom of speech and of association, freedom to travel abroad, freedom of inhumane imprisonment, and so on, may be true enough but it does not affect the logic of the argument about human rights.) Professor Cranston finds two distinguishing criteria: rights that are specific to a group of men only should not be called human in the sense of universal, and ideals (hoped-for eventual standards of attainment) should not be confused with rights, which should be respected and enforced now. The second objection to what has been promulgated seems to me the stronger.

A right to holidays with pay, indeed, applies only to one large group of people, employees. But formally one could easily universalise the statement and say, 'Everyone, if he is an employed person, has a right to holidays with pay'. It is not as special as the right of an ambulance driver to go through the traffic while other cars stop. I feel myself that there is only a minor objection to the inclusion of such specific rights in a universal declaration so long as they refer to very large groups (children, for instance). The real point is that these references are really to the situation of industrialised countries; the Universal Declaration and its offspring have been tilted in this direction and in that have become less genuinely universal. But the fact that they do not make such sense for the less developed countries belongs to the second objection, which I will examine in a moment.

That it is felt as a right to have some holidays sometime – and rather more than the one day a year enjoyed by Pippa in Browning's poem – would be hard to deny. This would be a welfare right and it would be universal. The catch is in the phrase 'with pay'. It could be argued that this depends on the state of profitability of an economy and that if you have to 'save up for the holidays', as our forefathers did, that is not so pleasant as being paid while you are away from work, but you have hardly been deprived of a universal right. Professor Cranston notes, fairly, that the rights of the Universal Declaration have often been spoken of as if they were just ideals, and that should not be so of a declaration or covenant of rights. I agree. But there is a great deal of difference between saying 'Primary education is a universal human right' and saying 'Primary education for every child is an ideal at which we should aim'. The latter lacks all the driving moral force of the former. And if the driving moral force for education is felt, as it indisputably is, the world over, can we deny that this is felt as a right?

I think the resolution of these difficulties must lie in the notion of attainability. Enforceable, which is the term Professor Cranston seems to prefer, goes a little too far. As Professor Ginsberg maintained, one can properly speak of rights before the stage of enforcement by law. Professor Cranston brings this idea in, as when he distinguishes between rights and ideals, but the way in which I would do it relieves us of the necessity (which I feel to be wrong) to make more than a distinction of convenience between civic and welfare rights. Education (at this stage universal primary education at least) is now felt to be a right because by and large it is attainable in the foreseeable future. Indeed we might have been very near to it now had it not been for the shockingly uncontrolled growth of the world's population (which means, disproportionately, a great growth in the proportion of the population that is of school age).

Much of the confusion in the Universal Declaration is, as Professor Cranston points out, because it uses the language of 'natural rights' in the traditional sense of that term. It was said to have been influenced very much by M. Jacques Maritain, whose confusions Miss Macdonald deals with in the paper to which I have referred. The education part of it would have been much less confusing had it begun: 'Since all human beings are in need of education to achieve the well-being of which they are capable, education is to be regarded as a universal human right that must now be realised everywhere to the greatest possible extent.' But, alas, in international organisations Rousseau-istic rhetoric is always likely to carry the day against dull Anglo-Saxon commonsense.

Only in a very special sense of the word 'nature' can one speak of natural rights. They are not innate in men in the sense that they are independent of society. Rights have no meaning apart from society. The concept of human nature comes in only in the sense that without the recognition of a given right, the fulfilment of which men are capable by their nature is frustrated when it need not be. This is what gives claims to rights their moral force.

It is no doubt this moral force behind the insistence that something be recognised as a right that has led people to conceive of some rights as absolute. When someone says, 'I have a right to this' there is indeed something of the absolute in his tone. Yet it does not take much reflection to see that in truth all rights are relative, and in the first place relative to one another. We may give initial respect to a statement about which a man feels strongly, but not an ultimate respect unless he can show us his reasons; and the reasons have often to be reasons for recognising this claim at the expense of others that would also seem to have their justifications. Instead of going into this at length and generally let me take just one important example, the rights of parents to choose the kind of education their children shall have.

The third clause of Article 26 of the Universal Declaration has an air of having been added as an afterthought. It reads: 'Parents have a prior right to choose the kind of education that shall be given to their children.' Now I do not know the facts but, knowing my United Nations and Unesco milieux, I would take a bet that this clause was not in the first draft but was added through the pressures of the confessional lobby. It is very confusing. What is the prior right prior to? To the rights of the electorate or the government to see that its funds are spent in the best way to serve the welfare of the community as a whole – which must entail not giving way to every minority claim as 'prior'? Prior to the right of society to prepare the next generation for common citizenship by that degree of common schooling that it thinks desirable? Prior to the rights of children afflicted with foolish or neglectful or bigoted parents? And how are the rights of one group of parents to be accommodated to the equal rights but differing claims of others? This has clearly not been thought out and allowed for.

Those who drafted our own Education Act of 1944 were more cautious. Section 76 of that Act says that regard must be had to the general principle that pupils are to be educated in accordance with the wishes of their parents, 'so far as is compatible with the provision of efficient instruction and training and the avoidance of unreasonable public expenditure'. Well, how much of the prior rights of parents is left after that? Professor Street[7] is no doubt right that this was drafted so as to protect public authorities from being legally answerable, should they not carry out the wishes of parents. But this is the kind of cautious drafting that misleads simple men. It is a bit too near political drafting, appearing to give large groups of voters what they want, but so hedging it round that they are most unlikely to get it. Parents have thought themselves entitled to public funds to send their children to schools of their choice, have taken authorities to court and have lost their money for their pains. They would have had as much, or as little, power, as groups of voters without this facing-both-ways clause.

It is of course right that the public authorities should be protected against unreasonable claims. As was said by a Frenchman (who for these purposes is usually known as Voltaire), England is a country of a hundred religions but only one sauce. What is fair for one religion is fair for another. But is every sect to have schools substantially paid for by public funds? The kind of school may also be chosen on grounds other than religious ones; but is the general public to pay for boys to go to private boarding schools because that is what some parents want, or does the clause mean only that they can send them if they pay for it themselves? In practice our policy is largely governed by the historical situation we have inherited. We hesitate to cancel rights (even if they are really privileges) in a way that would cause a sense of outrage and we try by the exercise of moderate good sense to preserve general fairness without giving way to the pressures of every individual or small group. This in general is how we conceive the public interest, and although it may lack clear-cut principle there is much to be said for it so long as in general we move in the right direction. But it is obvious that the supposed right of parents cannot be taken as an absolute, necessarily prior to the rights both of other particular parents and of the public in general.

What really is this 'right' of parents? It has been argued very reasonably by Mr H. J. McCloskey[8] that the right of a parent in relation to his children is that of a trustee. Their children are not their property, either physically or ideologically. We agree that it is reasonable that the children in a home of a given persuasion should in general be brought up within that framework of ideas. But if this is done in such a way as firmly to close their minds to other possibilities this is much more questionable. It militates against their right to their own self-development, to their rights to become reasonably autonomous persons. There are limits to the rights of trustees.

But the trustee argument, as McClosky says, can work the other way too. Parents do have to think very conscientiously about the way in which to provide the best education for their children. If the publicly maintained schools in general, or in a particular neighbourhood, are really bad ones then the claim that parents have not merely the right but the duty, if they can afford it or arrange it, to send their children to a school where they will get a reasonably good education, is a strong one. They will have to weigh very carefully the argument that they are buying privilege for their children against their duty as trustees to see that their children do have a good education. It could be said with some justice that to have parents who are deeply concerned about their children's education is an advantage to a community. But the point I am making is not that one answer rather than the others is always right (circumstances obviously make a great deal of difference) but that there can be no question of an absolute prior right of parents. It is, and must be, a matter of balance, and often a difficult one at that.

Rights then are in the first place to be seen in relation to societies and in the second as relative, not absolute. My third point follows naturally. Societies vary in their levels of development and relative priorities vary with these stages of development. For these reasons rights are to be seen, not as immutable, but as emergent, a description first used to me by my friend Dr Beeby, the former Director-General of Education for New Zealand and for a time Assistant Director-General of Unesco.

The idea that rights are emergent runs counter to the instincts of pure philosophers who, while admitting that some concepts seem more important in one state of society than another, tend to analyse them as such, as if they were existing permanently in the mind. They will undoubtedly say that there is a difference between a right and a claim that it be recognised. Women, for instance, must be held always to have had the right to be treated civilly and legally as persons equally with men, but it is only in comparatively recent times that the claim to the recognition of this right has been widely and strongly advanced and has gradually met with recognition. In pure logic it is difficult to deny that there is such a distinction between a right and the claim to its recognition, but I am uneasy about it because it seems to imply that a right may exist *in vacuo* and it seems clear to me that it can only exist in a society. The society may be in the first of Ginsberg's three stages, that is to say of intercourse between human beings without a durable society (though this is dangerously near the 'state of nature' that anthropologists would deny, primitive societies often being indeed highly complex structures); or it may be in his second stage, that of recognised but not yet legally enforceable rights; or in the third stage of rights acknowledged and backed by the law. But it is never in a social vacuum. Perhaps the one usefulness of the distinction is in the transitional stage when, as Ginsberg says, a moral right may be demonstrably justifiable though not yet widely recognised. In this transition people tend to say that a right exists though the claim to its recognition has not yet been conceded.

In practice no one hears of a supposed right until a claim is made for its recognition, and from this point of view the distinction between a right and a claim for its recognition is purely formal. I am perfectly prepared to concede the point (if only to save barren argument) and to use the phrase, 'rights are emergent', as shorthand for 'claims to rights are emergent', if that is preferred. Whether Crusoe had rights in relation to other people before Man Friday and the savages came seems to me a rather academic point.

We have seen that rights must be considered in relation to each other. The point I now want to make is that they emerge, in the sense that they are claimed, in relation to the possibility of realising them in practice if only people can be persuaded to do so. There is an interesting difference here between a need and a right, and often the paradox that the right is claimed more strongly as the need in fact grows less (just as revolutions break out, as has often been noted, not when people are oppressed the most but when a lightening of oppression has aroused their expectations of greater freedom still and a sense that they ought to, and could, have this).

Take a homely example. A very poor family may in truth need a car very much, but it can only sigh and say 'How marvellous it would be if we could afford a car!' The possibility is so remote that the question is just not worth raising. Then they do rather better in the world and say to themselves, 'Don't we really need a car for the shopping and to take the family off for a holiday?', though in truth they need it now less than when they were very poor. Then they rise still more in the world. They have a weekend cottage, their friends drop in for cocktails in their cars, and they say, 'We really *must* get a car'. If father retains his careful habits of his earlier days and won't get a car though they could afford it perfectly well, the family feels defrauded. They can afford it and they have a right to have one: why should he be so mean and stupid? The change to the imperative comes about first, because buying a car is now practicable, and secondly because they now feel a social compulsion which becomes almost a moral compulsion. This is an example on the material plane. If the father refused to contribute his parental supplement to a grant so that his sons and daughters could have a university education (he did well enough without one!) they would similarly feel on a non-material plane that they were being unjustly deprived of something to which they had a right. In other words, a right is something necessary to well-being that is attainable if people only will it to be so. All this happens in changing situations, of individuals and societies; and that is what I mean when I say that rights are to be seen as emergent.

This is what has happened in recent times in regard to education. Over the last hundred years or so it has been increasingly seen as necessary for industrialised societies to establish universal primary education and to extend and develop secondary and higher and further education. And, because of their increasing affluence it has become steadily easier for them to do so. From the point of view of the ordinary citizen his children's life-chances have come to depend more and more on education. Admittedly it has all been more complicated than was at first supposed: 'education is investment' is a slogan no longer naïvely accepted, education developed in relation to manpower planning is not the magic formula it only recently seemed to be (though we still have most troublesome graduate unemployment in many countries for lack of it) and above all the demand in many less developed countries has far outstripped the financial possibilities. Yet it remains true not only that a country cannot have a modern economy and a modern society without greatly extended education, but that the average man sees now how important it is and that as economies develop it is increasingly realisable. This is why they feel entitled to demand it as a right.

With these three initial points made about the nature of rights are we in a position to attempt at least a tentative definition? Basing ourselves on the analysis we have made so far, I would say:

> A right is a principle in virtue of which a claim is made on society on behalf of an individual, a group of persons or society as a whole, with a strong sense of moral compulsion behind it, and justified on the ground that unless it is recognised and acted upon a perfectly possible well-being will fail to be attained.

This, I repeat, is a tentative definition. One very important point I have not yet broached is the relationship – very important for those who attempt to justify rights that might look like privileges – between rights and duties. And then perhaps we may look again at the criteria we should use for testing the reasonableness of any claim (from our point of view especially in education) for the recognition and eventual legal establishment of a right.

The classic example of the correlation of rights with duties is a contractual one: if A has a right to be repaid money he has lent B then B has a duty to repay A the money he has borrowed from him. Life – and no less the question of the correlation of rights and duties – is rarely as simple as that! But the example is valid in principle. Broadening it, one might say that if an individual benefits from rights assured to him by society then he has a corresponding duty to act as a responsible member of that society, to help preserve it and improve it. (This, too, is over-simple. It must not be construed to mean that I have to seek to preserve every feature of my present actual society, but to be socially responsible, not anti-social, in my attitudes and behaviour.) The rationale of this correlation is clear. We cannot exist in isolation but depend for our welfare in each other, that is to say on being a member of human society. We wish to have the rights that membership of society gives us. Therefore we must logically desire the continuance of society. And that is only possible if men recognise their duty to society.

Laski took the view that rights were correlative with functions, and if it is held that you have a duty to perform such a function this comes to very much the same thing. We are quite happy, as I have said, that an ambulance should have the right of way over our own cars because we could not have an effective ambulance service for accidents if this were not so. The ambulance driver has a duty to get to the scene of the accident as quickly as possible. If he claimed right of way because he was out on a private spree that would be quite a different matter. It may be said in defence of special expenditure on the education of the specially able that if we do not give them such opportunities the community will not benefit from the fruition of their talents; and equally it may be said that if they do not recognise a duty to the community in return, but make it all redound to their private advantage, they are doing less than they should. As Laski put it, the claims made upon society, if they are to be justified, must be so because an identifiable public interest is involved in their recognition. Rights, he says, 'are correlative with functions. I have them that I may make my contribution to the social end.'

Now Benn and Peters do not feel that this is satisfactory.[9] They say there are rights we should consider justified that could not be defended in terms of a common good, 'if by that we mean an advantage in which every member of the community will have some share'. They say that even congenital idiots and murderers might properly be said to possess some rights though they make no contribution to the general good. Some would say that even animals have their rights. Personally I am not quite convinced by these objections. By the common good I would not mean an advantage in which every member of the community had a direct share. We most certainly benefit from living in a good society even though we do not personally and directly benefit from every example of its goodness. It is better to live in a compassionate society than a pitiless one even though we may not all need each particular kind of compassion (for instance to live in one that cares for its poor old people even though personally we may not need such assistance). And I am not sure that a man who has denied another man's right to life and would readily do so again does have a valid claim on society to respect his own life. The real argument against killing murderers is that to do so degrades the society that does it and is social conduct of a less civilised order than we should wish.

I would agree, however, that Laski invited attention to these rather special cases by suggesting that rights must always be correlative with functions. I think he was very near to the truth but stated it wrongly. Instead of saying that everyone who has a right must have it through contributing to a social function (his other term 'social end' is better) I would say that the recognition of the right is justified if society will be better for its being so. That such a maximising of the common good cannot be measured calculus-wise is, of course, true, but nor can many claims as to whether this society would be better than that. We can still discuss rationally and decide reasonably whether it would be or not.

Let me again take an example to illustrate this, and not least the point that there can be rational and persuasive discussion, based on the principle that the good of society is the relevant criterion for judging how far there is a right, even though there cannot be a final demonstration through the measurement of benefits. Let us look at students' rights to grants or, if they do not receive direct grants, to the indirect subsidies that public support of universities gives. I am not here discussing whether any particular claim is justified (for example a claim that grants to students have not kept pace with inflation, which should be capable of a statistical examination). I am concerned with the general principles involved.

On what grounds, in relation to rights, can students claim that they have a right to be supported while at a university, or to benefit from general public support of these institutions through capital and recurrent grants? We can say, first, that if there is not support for students through grants then selection will be not on grounds of merit but of the parental purse; and that is a wrong kind of selection. Whether there should be a contribution from those parents who can afford to make one is another question that is much argued. On the one hand not to demand this will not only mean a much bigger drain on public funds, but will simply subsidise the professional and middle classes who already have so much better chances of getting their young into the universities. On the other hand, it is said that a young man or woman now becomes a legal adult at the age of 18: surely he has the right to be considered no longer dependent on his parents at that age? Suppose, however, that we agree that university education should be without cost to the student and, if you like, without cost to his parents too, is there an unconditional right to such grants or is there an implied contract, a purpose for which the grants are made which must be reasonably well complied with if the claim to the right is to be maintained? There most clearly is, as Lord Annan said forcibly in the first Dimbleby Lecture which he gave for the BBC. Such a grant is not an unconditional gift. It is made for a purpose, the purpose of serious study. The first obligation of a student is to study.

One might have supposed that this was fairly obvious, yet if it were stated in the terms I have used at a conference of the National Union of Students I wonder whether it would be well received.

The great majority of students want their grants so that they can study at the university, fully accept the purpose of the grant and use it for that purpose. The majority of these are quietists and are not likely to be seen at a conference of the National Union of Students. Of those who do go to such conferences there are some, no doubt, who in their confused way, believe that their contribution to making a better society can lie in frustrating the teaching and administration of institutions of higher education. They have been a menacing minority who have got unrepresentative power in some of our institutions and, quite simply, they have no moral right to stay there. But how is it that they seem able, at least for a time, in the name of student rights to rally behind them a considerable number of 'activists' of whom it would still be unfair to say that basically they were not at a university or polytechnic in order to work?

I think that at the present time there is a paradox with which the socially minded student finds it very difficult to live. He belongs to a group in society which is at one and the same time both privileged and under-privileged. Students in higher education are undoubtedly privileged. They are supported by taxpayers' money to get qualifications which by and large will make their status and earning power superior to that of their exact contemporaries who are not in higher education. And at the same time they are temporarily underprivileged. They have less money in their pockets, and often considerably less, than their academically less able contemporaries who are at work. They are less obviously treated as fully adult. And they claim that they are fully adult, and have the right to be so treated. And if in addition they feel that the values of our present acquisitive society are wrong values and that 'alienation' is the mental disease of our time, why should not they try to change things at least in one sphere, the sphere of higher education where for the moment they are?

This is not the place for an examination of the practical difficulties that some of our institutions of higher education have experienced. I am con-cerned here with the question of 'rights'. Two things seem clear to me on one side of the question. One is that there is no 'right' to maintenance at a university or college that is not correlative with the duty to use it for the purpose for which society has afforded it, for study; and I would add that in my experience it is rare for university or college authorities not to take a pretty charitable view of a student who seems not to be going very hard. I should also add that in my experience there are fewer sheer idlers now than there were, at any rate in Oxford and Cambridge, in the years before the war. Secondly it should be said quite categorically, not that any student who protests about this or that has done anything he is not entitled to do, but that anyone who tries to stop teaching or tries to wreck the administra-tion has no more right to complain if he is expelled than any one has who voluntarily joins a club or society and tries to stop it from functioning. These two things, it seems to me, have not been asserted strongly enough.

On the other side of the question two things seem clear to me also. One is that if there is to be insistence that representations, whether it be about student life or studies, must be made through proper channels, then these channels must be seen to be real and effective. The second thing – and the two are related – is that students must be treated as adults. This does not mean that they are authorities on matters that they have come to learn, any more than an adult golfer is entitled to tell his club professional how to teach him. But there is a commoner view and in the latter case effect can be given to it if it is just ignored – you take no more lessons from that chap. The truth is that in reality the university student is nowhere like as free. He cannot just say that he will go somewhere else, or even in most cases change his teacher in the same place.

The complexities of the situation, with some attention to what rights a student does and does not have, are well brought out in an article that appeared in *Le Monde* of 3 April 1973, written by my former Unesco colleague, Professor Alfred Grosser. He was writing particularly about the protests of medical students in the University of Paris. He said:

> The State cannot free itself from concern about the social return on its investment in the universities. The right to the community's money that will permit you to study what you want for as long as you want cannot be unlimited. And the absence of all weeding-out, of all gradings in terms of merit, in short of selection, leads simultaneously to a denial of competence, and so to loss for the community.

But Grosser went on to say that although all this is true, and must be understood, it is too easy. Too often the game is not honest, because the cards are stacked. The universities are not always doing what they are supposed to be doing, the teaching is often neither useful nor culturally creative. As to outlets in jobs, if there clearly is a social need for more doctors and the government has spent money on things that are needed less than hospitals, the responsibility for the outcry when there is a brutal elimination of candidates for medicine is not just the students. This, it seems to me, is fairly put.

Although then in any particular case thinking out whether the claim to a right is justified can admit of no automatic answer, can we nevertheless come to a somewhat clearer understanding as to what in general the grounds for claiming that something is a right should be?

Benn and Peters, in rejecting Laski's view that rights were to be justified in terms of social functions, asked how we do make a decision when such rights conflict with others? Saying 'Maximise the common good' is no answer, for this is not something to be measured. 'Deciding in the light of the common good' is equivalent to judging impartially between claims in the light of the interests and needs of those affected. It is simply to apply the moral criteria they had discussed earlier in their book. This is right. But not all claims that may conflict with one another call themselves 'rights', and since there is something distinctive about that term I think there still are considerations that are distinctive when we have to balance such claims, and that we should pay especial attention to when a claim for something is made as a right.

Take first the tone of moral compulsion to which I have drawn attention as normally accompanying a claim for recognition of a right. If this were not present we might indeed doubt how strongly the claim was felt to be for a right. Yet in making a judgement we must be wary of it. People can easily persuade themselves that their rights are at stake. While we would not willingly produce a sense of outrage in our fellow citizens, just to bow before it is tantamount to saying that he who shouts loudest gets most. Somehow, while respecting deep feelings we have to take the heat out of the argument if we are to make a fair judgement. Strength and depth of feeling is an initial criterion but we must insist on something better and more widely sympathetic to others. Those who feel strongly about their particular rights often have too narrow a framework of reference. Those who value the secondary grammar schools may have a sense of outrage if a decision is made to 'go comprehensive'; but what about the sense of deprivation of those parents who are denied the grammar school for their children? The criterion here is consideration in terms of the whole constituency concerned.

This is another way of saying that we must get people to realise that no right is absolute. And that means, I am afraid, that they must, however strongly they feel, get the absolutist tone out of their voice. The criterion is reasonableness, not anger; though unfortunately wrongs are rarely righted in human society without that most Janus-like of qualities, commonly just and unjust at the same time, righteous indignation.

Is the practicability of giving effect to the claim a proper criterion, or can we say that we recognise a right in principle but of course cannot give effect to it yet? People who say this are nearly always suspect. It was, I believe, Bismarck who said that to accept in principle is to deny in practice. That was a share too cynical, though we must often feel that is all our assertion of rights has got for us. In fact when a reformer has secured an admission that something is right in principle he has won an important stage in his battle. A few more blasts on the trumpet (if this was just an excuse) and the walls of Jericho will fall.

In fact, as I have said, people do not on a wide scale claim something as a right unless it is on the verge of practicability. We do not say that we all have the right to go to the moon. When people deny that something is practicable they commonly mean, if other things that might be changed are not changed; and the question then is, which change will bring the greater benefit? It is quite certain, whatever is said about the universal right to primary education, that the really poor countries cannot afford it on present assumptions about the costs that must be incurred, and that some just a little nearer the economic take-off point could if they spent less on other things or developed their economy further. For the really affluent countries to say that they cannot afford a given proposed extension of their educational provision really means that they think other objects of extra expenditure are more important, as they may be; and those are the terms in which the discussion should be conducted.

In other words, practicability is a relevant criterion, but only if we force those who use it back on to their defences to test whether they are really sound.

When all that can be said about rights as a special kind of moral claim has been said, it is true that our criterion must be whether recognising the claim would or would not lead to a better society. That, I agree, is not a matter for precise measurement, but for reasoned and impartial discussion. For a right is a claim on society whose non-recognition would leave us with a less good society than we otherwise could have.

Chapter 8

The Concept of Equality in Education

Why do people say things like 'All human beings are born free and equal in dignity and rights'? They are born of parents and into societies that from the moment of birth offer them far from equal dignity and afford them far from equal rights. The idea that there is one almost infinitely short moment at birth when they are free and equal before they are affected by the fact that they are born of particular parents into a particular society is unreal. Even then they could hardly be said to be equal, for their genetic endowment has already been unequally determined. Yet phrases like the one I have quoted from the Universal Declaration of Human Rights clearly mean something, and something very important, to those who use them. What is this something about human equality? Taking the word at its face-value it is easy to demolish such a statement, to dismiss it as mere rhetoric. Yet the commitment of so many people over the centuries to the ideal of Equality cannot be understood unless we ask what it is that moves them and what its rational and explicable basis is. This seems to me a necessary prerequisite for understanding the demand for equality in education in some sense that is important and not nonsensical.

The distinction between language used descriptively and language used prescriptively is familiar enough. We know that in societies where there is discrimination against people because of their sex or colour of their skin they do not have equality in education or in general social status. We therefore say that the kind of language I have quoted is used only pre-scriptively, meaning not that they are but that they ought to be treated equally. But this does not go far enough. Those who use such phrases mean not only that they ought to be treated as equal but that in some sense they really are equal. What is this sense?

I don't think we can put aside the urge to find a rational and explicable basis for this passionate belief in what people call Equality. It may not be held by the majority of mankind, at least in an explicit way. It has been held by some of the rarest and finest spirits, and it has been obscurely but strongly felt by great masses of mankind who have not been treated equally. Is it only a matter of faith? Few people have felt it more deeply than R. H. Tawney or have been more capable of giving coherent and effective utterance to what they felt. Yet Mr Runciman quotes him[1] as admitting that reasons cannot be adequately given: it is in the end a matter of faith.

If a man affirms that his heart leaps up at the spectacle either of a society in which the common good is defined by the decisions of a totalitarian bureaucracy, or of one like – to mention only one example – the England of a century ago, where, in the unceasing struggle of individuals for personal gain, a conception of the common good cannot easily find a foothold, it may readily be admitted that no logic exists which can prove these exhilarating palpitations to be either right or wrong. One cannot argue with the choice of a soul; and, if he likes that kind of dog, then that is the kind of dog he likes.

I am not sure that a literal reading of this passage would express Tawney's final view. The passage itself is really saying, 'Turn your eye to the light and you surely must see what the implications of your view are. You can't really – unless you are both unfeeling and unthinking – hold the view you say you hold.'[2] At any rate it seems to me that we cannot just leave the question as to which society is better and which worse as a matter of taste or of faith; and, as I have hinted, I don't think Tawney would either. We are dealing with something that goes very deep in those who feel it, and often takes charge irrespective of surface logic. Nevertheless we cannot, it seems to me, avoid the task of, so to speak, uncovering and setting out the reasons for our faith.

A first clue may be found in the effects that purely descriptive studies of inequality have. They have often played a major part in lessening inequalities, just by revealing the facts. One thinks of the great series of reports of the middle of the last century in England. People were shocked into action by the accounts of the way women and children were treated in the mines, by the deplorable standards of health and housing which the poor had to put up with. And this tradition conditions. Amnesty International works against the unjust imprisonment of people simply for the non-violent expression of their views by getting and publishing the facts. The establishment of the facts produces a response in itself. Why should this be so, even in the minds of many who might be said actually to benefit from such ill-treatment of their fellow human beings?

There is a deep underlying feeling, even though such inequalities may seem to be to our advantage, that our fellow human beings should not be so treated, because they are our fellow human beings. Some people will go only part of the way with this argument. They will oppose cruelty or very positive ill-treatment, and may be persuaded to help to end it; but they would not take the move towards equality farther than that. They say: 'We share a common humanity and should not support practices or conditions that are clearly inhumane; but that is not to say that we favour equality.' This is a limited application of the principle of a common humanity, indicating chiefly what a human society must not do or allow to be done. Those who make our common humanity a more positive principle and a more universal one are more likely to invoke the general concept of Equality. Such people, as Tawney says,[3] are distinguished by their humanism, in the broad sense of that word, by their superb sense of the dignity of man. The language they speak has a universal application. Professor Raphael says[4] that the philosophical basis of the belief in a right to equality is Kantian, the categorical imperative to treat all individual men and women not merely as means but as ends in themselves. This does not mean, Professor Raphael points out, that all men are of equal worth in terms of utility to society or that there may not be some situations in which they may be considered as means to an end. But that they are not to be treated merely as means and have an equal right to be considered as ends in themselves is basic to the concept of Equality. It is this in which they are equal.

This is one of the very few matters in which I part company from Benn and Peters, whose *Social Principles and the Democratic State* has had such a marked influence in our time, not least in the professional preparation of teachers. They quote Hobhouse (*Elements of Social Justice*)[5] as an exponent of the argument for equality based on our common humanity:

As a matter of the interpretation of experience, there is something peculiar to human beings and common to human beings without distinction of class, race or sex, which lies far deeper than all differences between them. Call it what we may, soul, reason, the abysmal capacity for suffering, or just human nature, it is something generic, of which there may be many specific, as well as quantitative differences, but which underlies and embraces them all. If this common nature is what the doctrine of equal rights postulates, it has no reason to fear the test of our ordinary experience of life, or of our study of history and anthropology.

Benn and Peters don't accept this at all. When you strip away all the particular qualities in respect of which men differ, what is left? Only an undifferentiated potentiality, nothing clear and firm enough to justify a statement that in view of this common quality people should be treated equally. Even if they all need or desire something (food, for instance), they do so in different degrees and in different ways.

When we say all men are equal what we really mean, according to Benn and Peters, is that 'none shall be held to have a claim to better treatment than another, in advance of good grounds being produced'. This is necessary to satisfy the criterion of 'impartiality', which has been established as a necessary constituent of morality. This reformulation, they say, enables us to avoid the dilemma.

Benn and Peters, too, refer to Kant. They have argued that if in any particular matter we are to treat men differently this must be because of some factor relevant to the distinction we propose to make. We cannot ascertain this until we have considered their claims impartially. And this is much what Kant meant when he said we must treat humanity, in ourselves and others, as in every case an end and never solely as a means. This, however, does not mean that when every particular in men has been eliminated from consideration there remains something of value in itself, a fundamental 'humanity'.

I must admit that I find this argument rather thin. It would seem to me that Raphael was reasonable in making the conjunction that Benn and Peters reject. If you apply to humanity as a class the injunction that each member of it must be treated as an end in himself, logically you are imputing something common to all the individuals in the class. It might perhaps be said that all you have done is to apply something external, your injunction; but it would seem more convincing to say that your injunction derives from the fact that you have recognised something common in them that makes them a distinct class. That is why you apply your injunction to them and not, say, to animals.

Nor do I feel that the Benn and Peters' argument enables us to avoid the dilemma that they say exists. Their solution borders on tautology. Being just means being impartial, and being impartial means treating men equally unless we can advance good grounds for doing otherwise. But why should we be impartial? Because impartiality, in the sense of equality of consideration, is one of the criteria implied in the idea of morality. Quite so. And we apply it to all individual men because they are members of a class, humanity, in other words because of what they have in common.

I suspect that Benn and Peters were trying to get rid of the ghost of the 'state of nature' and of man's 'essential' nature in that state. But Hobhouse's argument stands on its own feet without that. Biologically man is a social animal and he is a distinct species. I find no more difficulty about man as a socio-biological species than I do about dogs as a species although there are many kinds of dogs and although no two of them, even of the same kind, are identical. There is no more difficulty about identifying man's common nature than there is with identifying other species'. Even if such a concept may be a little tricky on the borderlines it is serviceable, and indeed essential. You do not look for something that remains when every particular (such as whether you eat a lot or little) has been taken away. You look for characteristics that are common though present in different degrees. No zoologist hesitates to classify *Homo sapiens* as a species. We are increasingly used to the clumsy but necessary terms 'socio-biological', and man is a social animal. What men have in common socially as well as zoologically, or socio-biologically, is that they are all members of a single species, distinct enough to be so classified. That, at the straight descriptive level is what we mean when we speak of our common humanity. Benn and Peters would of course not deny this, but I do not think they draw the obvious inference from it as to our relationships with each other.

There is no doubt a prudential reason for treating men equally, as individual ends-in-themselves, or if you prefer the Benn and Peters word, impartially. It makes for a more stable and generally accepted society, though in the short run (and sometimes for rather a long short run) a privileged minority can hold its fort. But there is also a reason of principle, and this does rest in the end on the idea of our common humanity. Let us look at this first.

The tradition that in some important sense men are equal goes back a long way, and this surely cannot be lightly brushed aside. In the West generally it goes back to the later Stoics; in Rome to Cicero. It links up with the idea of natural law, of natural justice and of equity. The same feeling that in some important sense men are equal is present in some of the world religions: in Christianity (all men are equal in the sight of God, all men are brothers in Christ) and in Islam, though not perhaps in Hinduism because of the dominant-caste idea.

However, such traditions of thinking about our common humanity do not carry implications that men should be equal in goods or in social status. The great majority of Christians believing that all men are equal in the sight of God have not been troubled by this; St Paul accepted slavery. Nor were there implications that men were equally good (what sense would that have made of the Day of Judgement?). To someone like myself, reared in Christian socialism, it came as something of a shock to realise that the social 'reactionaries' of my youth, like Dean Inge, had just as good a claim to be considered Christians as people on the other side such as Bishop Gore and William Temple and my own Nonconformist socialist father. I was similarly surprised, and at first shocked, to realise that the leaders of the slave-owning South in the American Civil War were just as strong Christians as people in the free North. So one must not misread this tradition of thought. The belief that all men are in some important sense equal is not necessarily social egalitarianism.

Yet there was bound to be a carry-over. In Western Christianity, once the hopes of an almost immediate Second Coming faded, there were bound to be those who asked whether we should not build the Kingdom of Heaven here on earth. For all the hierarchic structure of the mediaeval Catholic Church and the firm alliance it made, not least because of its own property interests, with the established social order, this egalitarian, utopian strain keeps coming out. In the Peasants' Revolt of the fourteenth century in England we remember not only Wat Tyler but the priest, John Ball. Luther at the time of the Reformation was faced with a cruel dilemma. He depended on the support of powerful princes and his fateful decision to condemn the Peasants' War in Germany settled the social and political role of Lutheranism for all time. It was to be quietist, respecting the powers that be and obedient to them. This was not the same in other branches of Protestantism. The Christian socialists and the nonconformist Christian trade unionists were a kind of left wing of the churches, conscious of a social role, not dissimilar (though in a different setting) to the movement that developed in France with Péguy and after him the worker-priests. In England a strong strand in Anglo-Catholicism made a link between the two. In other words the tradition that in some important sense men were all equal was not simply other-worldly. Without being really revolutionary it took on for many people a strong social tone and tinge. What was it that was common to all men and in what way were they to be treated as equal here on earth?

What all men share is simply *the human condition* and, unlike other species, consciousness of it. What that basic equality implies is, as Sidney Hook puts it,[6] not identity of treatment but equality of *concern* for every person. And here in human society, now.

The human condition? Is not this rather general, rather abstract? It is general, because it is universal; but far from being merely abstract it has most fundamental practical consequences once you grasp it and act upon it. It has never been better put than it was in the famous words of Colonel Rainborough in the confrontation between the Levellers in the army and the property-defending Ireton, son-in-law of Cromwell, at the time of the Civil War and the struggle about the kind of England there was to be after it. To the argument that property, unequally held, was the guarantee of social stability, Rainborough answered that in the most basic thing of all, the human condition, men were equal and had an incontrovertibly equal stake.

> The poorest he that is in England hath a life to live as the greatest he; and therefore truly, Sir, I think it's clear that every man that is to live under a government ought first by his own consent to put himself under that government; and I do think that the poorest man in England is not at all bound in a strict sense to that government that he hath not had a voice to put himself under.[7]

The Levellers were asking for political equality. The extension to economic and social equality was a logical one, and the Diggers of this period foreshadowed it. But it is the ground of the claim, not the extent of the claim, that concerns us at the moment. Essentially this is that each of us has one life to live. There is no reason to suppose that your life means less to you than my life does to me, and the only ground of appeal from me to you to live loyally in a common society with me is a recognition of that quite fundamental equalness. The basic human condition, of being born, having only one life to live, and dying, is a condition in which we are all equal. The recognition of this equality in respect of the condition of all men goes very deep indeed. It is really what Hobhouse meant, and I do not think it can be ignored. It is this and not some residual characteristics that might remain when we have shed our particular qualities that gives us our sense of a common nature, a life and a condition that we equally share. It is this that makes being treated without concern so bitter and that often makes the struggle for equality so passionate.

Equality of concern does not mean identity of treatment. As Benn and Peters say, you do not give identical treatment to a sufferer from diabetes and a sufferer from rheumatism, but you should have an equal concern for the health of them both. This combination of an equal concern for all the members of a society with the greatest variation of its expression, since individuals have different needs and different potentialities, is, as John Dewey said,[8] the essence of democracy. The consequences for education (to which I will come in a moment) are profoundly important and should be our cardinal guiding principle whether we sit in the administrator's office or work directly with children and students in the classroom.

Indeed, the realisation that unequal treatment is necessary for unequal cases to restore the balance and attain equality is as old as Aristotle. This is the basis of the case for spending more on the handicapped, and it may well be on the gifted child than we spend on the average child. But cause has to be shown. The principle does not justify inequalities where the differentiating criterion reveals a lack of equal concern. In a family the strongest is not allowed to grab the most food. That would be an infringement of the principle of equal concern. But if one child needs a special diet and this costs more than is spent on any other child in the family, the principle of equal concern not only allows but demands it.

The principle of equal concern does not imply identity of endowment. Indeed those who understand it realise that it means apparent inequality of treatment precisely because we are not all equally endowed, any more than we are equally healthy. I would only note that we must be on our guard against those who advance this consideration for their own advantage. Let us assume for the sake of argument that Jensen is right in saying that the average intelligence of black Americans is lower than the average intelligence of white Americans, it still would not follow (nor does he say it would) that all black Americans should go to black schools and all white Americans to white schools. The idea of equal but separate may be honestly advanced, but it should be looked on with some suspicion. It may mean that we want to be separate precisely because we do not consider others our equals, as the Supreme Court rightly decided about segregated schooling in the United States and as world opinion long ago decided about apartheid in South Africa.

What is the criterion of fairness when differentiation of treatment or of status is advocated or defended? One of the really original ideas in contemporary social philosophy is that put forward by Professor Rawls of Harvard to elucidate this question. There are inequalities that some people defend on the ground that they are just (it may be just to reward superior merit or an exceptional contribution to society or to meet a special need) whereas others may think the defence of the inequality spurious. The test as to whether this is just would be that, before you knew whether you would be the rewarded or the penalised person, you would acclaim the inequality as fair, and stick to your decision if you found that you turned out to be the disadvantaged. This is not just fanciful. There have not been many slaves who said that slavery was just – and incidentally it is a little surprising that Plato, who was, it is said, captured by pirates and would have been sold into slavery had he not been ransomed by his friends, did not reflect on the arbitrariness with which people often find themselves in one category rather than another. Certainly parents of very young children can say in advance whether they think a selective system of secondary schools is proper and fair. But how do they feel when their boy or girl fails to get into the grammar school? If they stick to their view that this division according to supposed merit is just then they are being logical; but it seems to me that the embattled defenders of the grammar schools are the parents who have got their children there, not those who have not. The defence would be more impressive if it were the other way round.

Mr W. G. Runciman[9] has a thorough discussion of Rawls's criterion and broadly accepts it. But in discussing inequalities of status, to be justified or not justified, he makes an interesting distinction of his own between people who are praised and people who are respected. Inequalities of status in a just society, he says, would only be defensible where they could be plausibly shown to be inequalities of praise. We may praise a Beethoven or a Shakespeare and, assuming our praise to be well-founded, the fact that we praise a dustman less does the dustman no injustice. But if we respect less, as men, those who make no claim to genius there is injustice. A group in society deprived of respect does therefore suffer from a hurtful inequality.

There is something attractive in this idea. Clearly we need a distinction of something like this kind. But the words placed in antithesis do not seem to me quite to hit the mark. In Shaw's play *The Doctors' Dilemma*, where the problem is to make a just decision as to whether to save the brilliant painter who is a bad character or the very ordinary chap who is a good one, do we praise the painter Dubedat for his painting and dispraise him for his character, or do we respect him for one and fail to respect him for the other? It seems to me that we praise and respect him for his painting and neither praise nor respect him for his character.

I would rather suggest a distinction between unequal status gained by a quality, or from successful discharge of a function we admire, and what I would call generalised unequal status. Thus most of us (to take familiar examples) would not resent somewhat higher rewards than the average going to excellence in something society values, whether it be high skill in football or greatness as a writer; but when a whole group or class achieves and maintains a status that gives disproportionate rewards and respect (such as mere inheritors of wealth or titles) we feel very differently, unless of course our whole social philosophy is Burkean.

Even what I have just written is really not critical enough, for we can have a strong sense of injustice even where there is merit in those who are favoured if this leads to a generalised and quasi-permanent status. This was shown very forcefully in Michael Young's *Rise of the Meritocracy*,[10] where the superior general status of those who are more intelligent and who work hard ('IQ plus effort = merit') was felt as intolerably unjust by the others. The reason was that men were not treated as men, but merely as brains that worked, and that this discrimination was accomplished fairly made things worse rather than better, for it left the rest of the people with no consoling excuse for their unequal treatment. Brains and effort are very important; but it is not brains and effort alone that make a man. To give generalised high status on these grounds alone, though it seems 'fair', is in fact unjust. It ignores the basic equality of man; or, to put it in another way, it makes a generalised exception to equality on grounds that are only in part relevant. The second part of such a statement would satisfy the criteria of Benn and Peters. The first part of it is one that I would wish to make as well, for it is what has motive force, and with justification.

The prudential reason for recognising that in a real sense men are equal I touched upon when I said that since each of us has one life to live and there is no reason to suppose that your life means less to you than my life does to me, the only ground of appeal I have to you to live loyally in a common society with me is a recognition of that fundamental equality between us. It is a crude view that holds that societies are held together by force. Force, or the threat of it, is necessary in any society to restrain evil-doers. Law would not be respected by them if there were no sanctions behind it. But what really holds societies together is common consent. We want to live in societies, and indeed we have to. We want the benefits of living in a society for ourselves, and we soon understand that this is dependent on our recognising reciprocal obligations to others in it. A society may be held together by force and fear, reinforced by controlled persuasion, but the moment the threat from a tyrant is lifted he is liable to be overthrown. Ideologies may for a while persuade the mass of people to accept their suppression. As the success of Communist oligarchies shows, modern methods of communication make this easier than it used to be. But dissidence will not die and sooner or later there will be a decisive breakthrough. Religions have often served the same kind of end. Do they, I wonder, still sing that absurd hymn about the rich man in his castle, the poor man at his gate, and claim that God made them high and lowly and ordered their estate? Of all the religions, Hinduism has the most superbly built-in device, in its caste system, for making the lower orders believe that they themselves are responsible for the unequal status from which they suffer. But Gandhi, and their own leaders, broke through on behalf of the untouchables; and caste cannot long survive industrialisation. The case for a social as well as a political democracy is that although it may look weaker it is in the long run a stronger, because a more acceptable, system than any other. Those societies now that are not in any sense democratic have to pretend that they are, for just that reason.

Cicero said that, apart from his fellow citizens who might not like him, a man had as many enemies as he had slaves. A society is the more likely to cohere, without the employment of force that degrades it, the stronger the consensus, the sense of the social bond freely accepted by its members. A really firm democracy can even deliberately install a temporary dictatorship in times of danger when decisions must be quickly taken and firmly carried out, and still revert to its norms when the danger has passed. Cincinnatus was called to be dictator and afterwards contentedly went back to his plough. Sparta was ultimately a weak, not a strong state, ruled by fear of the Helots. A section of the inhabitants, and especially a large one, that feels it is being denied political or social equality without good cause shown, is always a threat to a regime. 'One is to count for one and for no more than one' is the practical maxim for a strong democracy. This is the prudential argument for equality.

The prudential argument for equality is not, however, the most important one. Those who hold to this belief do so in the end because they believe that it makes for a finer society, as Pericles held to Athenian democracy, quite irrespective of whether they were stronger or weaker in war. This comes through very strongly in Tawney's classic *Equality*. The real argument against a society based on inequality is that it betrays the best in human nature. Scorn is not too strong a word to use for his feeling about a society that values material wealth above the good ends to which it should be put, that has little social conscience and believes that the resultant of the acquisitive scramble will serve instead, that is content with what Professor Galbraith has called private affluence and public squalor (Tawney said the same but used the Latin, *Privatim opulentia, publice egestas*.)[11] Nor is Tawney taken in by that meretricious substitute, Equality of Opportunity. Indeed at this his scorn rises to its height. No doubt the individualism of the past century and a half had broken down many legal barriers and had liberated the energies of the bourgeoisie. But what a social philosophy! I have quoted the passage[12] before, elsewhere, and I do not apologise for quoting at least part of it again:

> It is possible that intelligent tadpoles reconcile themselves to the inconveniences of their position, by reflecting that, though most of them will live and die as tadpoles and nothing more, the more fortunate of the species will one day shed their tails, distend their mouths and stomachs, hop nimbly on to dry land, and croak addresses to their former friends on the virtues by means of which tadpoles of character and capacity can rise to be frogs. This conception of society may be described, perhaps, as the tadpole philosophy. . . . And what a view of human life such an attitude implies! As though opportunities for talent to rise could be equalized in a society where the circumstances surrounding it from birth are themselves unequal! As though, if they could, it were natural and proper that the position of the mass of mankind should permanently be such that they can attain civilization only by escaping from it! As though the noblest use of exceptional powers were to scramble to shore, undeterred by the thought of drowning companions!

Tawney wrote that in 1931. Is it out of date in 1975? One might have hoped that it had at least begun to be so with the more socially progressive and compassionate conservatism of some of the post-war Conservative leaders. But their present leader, Mrs Thatcher, has made this same 'equality of opportunity' the slogan of her party in the attempt to get it back to power. No doubt if she were successful she would not scrap all the social services, but the tendency is clear: less positive action by the government for the community as a whole and more reliance on individual thrust, with the prizes for the most thrustful. It reveals the same outlook as that of the Lord Birkenhead whose philosophy of glittering prizes for the thrustful excited Tawney's contempt in 1931. It appeals more to resentments than to serious argument, and it is a long way from the kind of conservatism that puts the country and the community first and material individual ambition second.[13]

The resentments to which it appeals are those of the vigorous person who feels himself hemmed in by 'bureaucrats'. Good men as well as greedy men can be hemmed in by petty restrictions and the community can suffer from it. The choice is between going back to the days when there were few restraints, except the police, on persons who put the making of their fortune above the welfare of their fellow men, and controls to save us from private affluence and public squalor, but controls that are democratic and participatory, not bureaucratic.

The only respectable argument for the Birkenhead–Thatcher philosophy is that, however deplorable it may be, giving free range to the acquisitive drives of the thrustful will result in more public benefit than restraining them. This way more wealth will be created and in the end the community will benefit. There are times in the history of societies, especially when legal barriers have stood in the way of the initiative of a whole class, when this could be argued with some plausibility. It was a commonly held view in the first two-thirds of the nineteenth century and the increase in wealth by the bourgeoisie in England and France lent strength to the argument. But what a price was paid in terms of both human misery and of vulgarity, as critics from both left and right – both Marx and Balzac – saw. It is a much less plausible argument in the days of powerful, and necessarily 'bureaucratic', multi-national companies in which individualism, too, is 'out'. The real question, again as Tawney said, is whether you rate higher accumulating wealth or devoting wealth to civilised uses. What is called 'equality of opportunity', as it is certain to be interpreted, is very different from the principle of equality and the ideal of the good community as more important than individual gain. In the end, what an essentially vulgar view of man it gives!

I said 'as it is interpreted' because if you really wanted to give everybody an equal opportunity you would have to intervene to correct the inequalities of circumstance, which is just what these exponents of 'equality of opportunity' resent. You would have for instance to insist on comprehensive schools, so that people could start their adult life on a somewhat more equal footing rather than having, if there is not only a selective public system but a private and expensive system as well, a tremendous handicap to overcome if they are not in the privileged group. This is not at all what Mrs Thatcher means. As Minister of Education she slowed down the movement to comprehensive schools. 'Equality of opportunity,' as it is interpreted, means freedom to drive ahead for the strongest and ablest without a major attempt to care for the weaker and less able, or even to see that they at least start reasonably equal in circumstance, as is demanded by those who make the principle of equality their guiding idea.

The example I have just given shows how intimate is the connection between people's general social outlook and their views on policy in education. It is to the educational implications of the idea of Equality that I would now like to turn. But before coming to questions of general policy I would like to note that these ideas bear not only on what a Minister of Education does but on what teachers in their classrooms do. This is not always seen by students preparing to be teachers, who are apt to say, 'This theory is all very well, but what has it to do with our daily work?'

This question was in fact put to me by a student in a seminar held following a lecture that had been given by Professor Peters on Equality. I said, 'Do you think a teacher should treat the children in her class equally?' 'Of course,' she replied, a little too quickly. 'Does everyone agree?' I asked the seminar. 'Well, not quite,' said someone. 'Not literally. If a child in your class needs extra help, say with his reading, you should give it him even if he does get more than the average share of your attention.' 'And do you think the others in the class would resent that as unfair?' 'No, not if they saw he did need it and knew that you would help them similarly if they needed it.' So we soon reached the point that equality did not mean literally equal shares, but equality of concern; that you had to treat unequals equally if you were to get equality – that exceptions to apparent equality were to be justified, and would be understood, if the reasons were relevant to making people in reality more nearly equal. And so on to other very practical matters, such as the justification for risking 'playing favourites' when some child needed the extra glow of approbation, though really having favourites was certain to be resented. I hope the point got home: that theory in education, whether in policy or teaching, is not some useless abstract game but thinking about your concepts and assumptions so as to make the practice as sound as you can make it.

Take the question of equality of treatment in the matter of punishments. Should a punishment for the same offence be different for different boys? Personally I think that there is rather more to be said for a 'tariff' than is fashionable now. There still is something in the old idea, 'That was the offence, that was the price to be paid if I was found out, and the slate is now wiped clean.' Purging the offence is a most necessary ingredient in retaining the offender's self-respect. 'He is a beast, but a just beast' as one schoolboy once said of a famous headmaster. But I would keep this tariff principle for fairly minor offences that have to be penalised in the interest of the school community. It could be dangerously insensitive carried beyond that. Fortunately corporal punishment is much less often resorted to than it used to be. The effect of it notoriously varies from boy to boy. Some would prefer it to really wounding sarcasm and declare in later life, possibly with truth, that it never did them any harm. That is not true of others, who may be just as courageous and spirited but feel it to be an outrage on their dignity as persons. Something depends on the social background and its expectations: an American boy who was caned in an English school would almost certainly not stand for it, nor would his parents. But what would the rest feel if he got off because he was an American? I would see only one way out: tell him that because he comes from a country where they do not have corporal punishment he can be given an alternative, and that the school will be told that that is the reason, acceptable in the special circumstances to the headmaster, and then let him choose. I think I know which he would choose – and that would be as near to equality as one could get.

There is no easy or automatic application of even the best-thought-out general principles to particular cases; yet we must think them out as best we can. What is certain is that if a teacher or headmaster is known to have equal concern, even though he applies apparently unequal measures, that will be seen to be so and be understood. A school and its teachers can do relatively little to make up for either genetic inequalities or inequalities in parental love and support. But they can do something. The great need of all of us is to feel that we are valued for something that we can contribute or something that we are. The idea of equality does not depend on a sup-position that all people are equally gifted but on the belief that it is equally important to help everyone discover and use the gifts he has. A faith in the ungifted child will sometimes create the reality that justifies the faith.

The individual teacher and the individual school, however, must operate within a framework that is socially and to a large extent politically laid down. This is bound to be so whatever the prevailing social philosophy may be. It would still be true if a society decided to have no public system of education at all, for that would reflect a view of a good society as one in which the government does little or nothing for the general welfare. This point is little understood, especially by the defenders of private schools. No school can be entirely private. Whether you are for them or against them, private schools are bound to be a matter of public concern. A short-run distinction between the terms social and educational is acceptable enough, as when one says that parents send their children to private schools for social rather than educational reasons, or on the contrary for educational rather than social reasons (because although they would otherwise prefer a public school those in the neighbourhood are just not good enough). But beyond this level of discourse the antithesis will not hold. The education of all its future citizens is something that must be the concern of any national community.

In the earlier days of the controversy about comprehensive schools the defenders of the selective system often said of their opponents, 'They want comprehensive schools for social, not educational reasons,' and said it with an air of having clinched the matter. In a press statement (with which some of their number were by no means happy) the Australian Headmasters Conference held in 1975 accused those who questioned the large subven-tions given to these schools from public funds as engaged in 'social engineering', an unfair term because it implied that those who were con-cerned about the interest of the whole community were manipulating human lives as one manipulates pieces of metal, and just in the interest of some doctrinaire view. The real ground of defence for such schools must be different, that they can be shown to contribute to the total social welfare and therefore merit general community support. The case would need to be carefully argued, but so far as my acquaintance with Australian education goes it could be argued at least for the time being, and especially if such schools came increasingly within the public orbit. In England the short answer to those who say that those who defend comprehensive schools do so on social rather than educational grounds is simply: 'Of course. What better grounds could there be?'

There are indeed other things to be taken into account, such as whether a comprehensive school is, or need be, poorer than a selective one; but I would give the short answer first if only to clear some of the nonsense out of the way.

One could also support the view that the social argument is not to be brushed aside from, so to speak, the other end of the spectrum. Mr Christopher Jencks argues[14] that if schools in the United States were completely desegregated the reduction of cognitive inequality between black and white Americans would be slight. He says that the case for desegregation should not be argued in academic terms. The right argument is different. 'If we want a segregated society, we should have segregated schools. If we want a desegregated society, we should have desegregated schools.' I think Jencks is absolutely right.

The role of the community school has been very important in American social history. Professor Freeman Butts, feeling that there has recently been an erosion of faith in public education as one means for building a sense of national community, has written an eloquent restatement of this ideal:[15]

> A public school serves a public purpose rather than a private one. It is not maintained for the personal advantage or private gain of the teacher, the proprietor or the board of managers; nor does it exist simply for the enjoyment, happiness or advancement of the individual student or his parents. . . . Rather, the prime purpose of the public school is to serve the general welfare of a democratic society, by assuring that the knowledge and understanding necessary to exercise the responsibilities of citizenship are not only made available but actively inculcated. . . . Achieving a sense of community is the essential purpose of public education.

I would substitute 'an' for 'the' in the last sentence of this statement, because I agree with Matthew Arnold that the prime purpose of education is not to make a man a good citizen, or a good Christian, or a gentleman, but to enable a man to know himself and his world.[16] But, certainly, part of that world is the society in which he will live, and with that one amendment Freeman Butts is surely right.

In England the cruder disparities in our educational system were modified by the 1944 Act. Up to that time they had been glaring; and the issue was indeed not narrowly educational, but social. When Mr H. A. L. Fisher had come forward after the First World War with an Education Bill that now looks modest enough, the Federation of British Industries issued a statement saying that its proposals for compulsory schooling till 14 and a measure of day-release from work after that would be something, except in terms of very gradual development, that industry would be quite unable to bear. Tawney at once took up this challenge.[17] He said that of course every extension of the school-leaving age or the like involved a certain amount of industrial readjustment, but the idea that industry depended so much on juvenile labour that it would be ruined by such a step had no evidence to support it. But the real difference was one of belief.

Those who think that men are first of all men have no premise in common with those who think, like the authors of the Federation's Memorandum, that they are first of all servants, or animals, or tools. . . . Stripped of its decent draperies of convention, what it means is that education is to be used, not to enable human beings to become themselves, nor to strengthen the spirit of social solidarity, nor to prepare men for the better service of their fellows, nor to raise the general level of society; but to create a new commercial aristocracy, based on the selection for higher education of 'the more promising' children of working-class parents from among the vulgar mass, who are fit only to serve as the cannon fodder of capitalist industry.

It is a measure of the progress we have made, modest though it may be, that those seem strong words now. They were an accurate exposure of the hard-faced men too prevalent in British industry at that time. The tone of voice, and to some extent the attitudes, have changed. But the passage still goes to the heart of the matter. If you want a society where men are regarded as men, equally regarded though they may not be equally able or clever or rich, you will legitimately demand that education shall fit into and prepare for such a society.

Chapter 9

Three Ways of Thinking about Education

It is easier to check whether one's thinking is straight in a subject like mathematics than in education. Mathematics has its internal logic and is abstracted from everyday reality. Education is rooted in the mixed situations that confront us in daily life and uses concepts that derive from a variety of disciplines. Each of these disciplines brings to the study of education concepts that are illuminating but may also be distorting. Thus economics has contributed greatly to our study of education in its public aspect, but some of the terms that it has brought over are not happy ones in their new context. To speak of education as an industry, or to apply notions of 'productivity' as if its purpose was to deliver a priced output to a market in relation to so many man-hours of teacher labour, is to distort thinking and policy making. The economist of education must be an educationist as well as an economist, and of course the best are.

Commonsense in educational thinking, as in educational practice, consists very largely, not in setting up as the enemy of theoretical studies, but in understanding how far in every situation there is a need to call in one kind of study to supplement another. This is the parallel in the conceptual sphere to what is obviously necessary in educational practice. Let me make my point first by reference to practical situations.

A colleague of mine was much involved in a Unesco-supported experiment in science education in Nigeria. There was a pilot scheme that had been tried out in a limited number of schools. It was tried in the first grade, continued with these children when they entered the second grade and at the same time started with the children in the new first grade. This involved a steadily increasing momentum, with new materials each year for each successive grade and a new group of specially trained teachers. Suddenly the politicians, believing the scheme to be a good one, wanted to hurry everything up, and to increase the number of schools several times over. The first year's work had been successful and nobody wanted to go slow for the sake of slowness. But the whole effort might have been discredited and a failure taken the place of a probable success, because the necessary new and additional materials and the necessary number of new teachers trained to understand the experiment and how to conduct it were not there. In other words political drive (which we can call idealism perhaps in this case) without thinking out the logistics could have been fatal. The first thing to do was to ascertain whether it was possible to speed up supplies and trained teachers and only then to discuss whether it would be wise to change the planned rhythm of the experiment. To raise such a question would be second nature to the administrator. It is not second nature to a politician, though he may often be brought to see the point. In other words there were two ways of looking at things here and only strongly asserted commonsense could reconcile them.

Let me give another example from our own educational history, this time where the politicians and the administrators were both wrong and foolishly over-rode those who understood better what education was about and what would be the consequences for learning and teaching if they had their way. Before we had a public elementary school system, grants were made to the existing non-state schools for ordinary children and Parliament wanted to ensure that grants were made in accordance with ascertainable good results. What could sound more reasonable? (We often hear the same sort of cry now, and it is never possible to say that it is wrong, only that wrongly understood it might wreck the very purpose of the grant.) So we had the system of 'payment by results' which has been anathema to teachers ever since. Under the influence of Robert Lowe (the minister, as we should now call him, who was in charge), government grants to elementary schools were to be given only after examination of individual schoolchildren by the inspectors, who also were to check the numbers enrolled and attending. As the most eminent of the inspectors, Matthew Arnold, pointed out, this made the teachers, pressed by their headmasters and headmistresses (and their salaries depended on it), rely on mechanical processes rather than intelligence and learn the ways to swell the role and get the children through the tests. Five years after the introduction of this Revised Code, as it was called, the intelligence, spirit and inventiveness of the children were clearly falling off. Lowe had prided himself that the new Code would be either efficient or cheap, or both. Efficiency and economy might certainly seem to be things at which politicians and administrators should aim, but thinking in this dimension only did damage to our elementary education from which it took many long years to recover. Only a few years ago, I heard an economist whom I would not ordinarily accuse of failing to understand educational values say, 'What's wrong with payment by results?'. If he had known his educational history a little I think he might have avoided this professional deformation coming from his uncomplemented parent discipline.

We are in this kind of difficulty in educational thinking, that there has to be a double play. On the one hand there must be greater analytical specialisation, the working-out of educational theory in relation to its various parent disciplines, philosophy, sociology, history, psychology and economics. Only thus can intellectual rigour and respectability be obtained. But on the other hand, simply because education is such a multidimensional thing, exclusive reliance on any one of these theoretical frameworks, either for our thinking or in practice, is almost bound to distort. If the specialist himself is not aware of this (and it might be argued that to be too conscious of it would prevent him from pressing to extract all the possible virtue from the aspect of things with which he is concerned, though I really doubt this), then the teacher, the headmaster and headmistress, and the interested public must be. They must be able to understand what the specialists are doing and what the bearing of their work is, but they must see the total picture in the light of a commonsense that is not a poor substitute for real knowledge and still less a cover for prejudice – but an indispensable ingredient of serious educational thought.

In this chapter I would like to look at three ways of thinking about education out of the many there are, and to say something about their nature and why alone they can rarely 'give us the answers'. These three ways are the philosophical, the pedagogical and the administrative.

Philosophy was once a very wide word, indeed almost all-embracing. It was thought that it gave knowledge, chiefly by reasoning about our experience and about the nature of things and of 'Reality'. Indeed, until the eighteenth century it included science, which was commonly known as natural philosophy. During the eighteenth and nineteenth centuries the sciences gradually differentiated themselves from philosophy, but the word was still connected in men's minds with a kind of knowledge. There was a tendency to believe that the kind of knowledge it gave was 'higher' than that given by the sciences. The temptation among philosophers to create a system of thought which gave a rational knowledge of the world and which, being rational, was 'real', was still strong. At the risk of oversimplifying one can say that in the last half-century the claim of philosophy to be in any sense a corpus of knowledge or to establish a system of 'higher' truth has been given up by philosophers.

The notion that philosophy is a body of knowledge went out decisively with Schlick and the Vienna School of philosophers of the first quarter of the present century. Schlick suggested that we should use the adjective more and the noun less, that study of all subjects should be as philosophical as possible but that we should give up all notions of philosophy as a subject with its own body of knowledge. But what was it to be philosophical about a subject of study? To explain its assumptions, to analyse its concepts, to give justification for its procedures and conclusions. But should not a writer or teacher in any field do this for himself? He certainly should. But questioning of this kind may be described as a technique for which training is desirable and the systematic application of it is to some extent a specialised job. Most philosophers tend to be concerned with the philosophy of something, political philosophy, moral philosophy, the philosophy of science, or whatever it may be; and, of course, of education. So they have a double affinity, with their disciplinary area and with philosophy as it is now understood. It is also true that there has been a reaction from the logical positivism that was part of their outlook; and this has been associated with a degree of rehabilitation of metaphysics. Nevertheless I think this short account is broadly right.

What philosophers of education have concerned themselves with during the last fifteen years or so has been in line with these general tendencies: to examine the assumptions, the concepts and the justifications for general positions taken in educational discussion. The usefulness of this cannot be gainsaid. Its effect on discussion about education in this country has been marked: we now tend to expect a clarity, a power of discriminating, that was much less common before there became the kind of school of philosophers of education that we have now. Anyone concerned with education, be he teacher, research worker, administrator or seriously interested member of the public, who does not know something of this work and has not to some extent caught the habit of this kind of questioning will be the poorer for it. Yet – and Professor Peters has insisted on this point – philosophy of education cannot, and does not claim to, 'give the answers'. It should affect the way we think about education. It does not give ready-made solutions to any problem. So we can say, not as a criticism of this kind of theoretical work but as clarification of its role, that it is both very necessary and, from a practical point of view, insufficient.

The two previous chapters in this book, although I am not a professional philosopher, deal with questions that philosophers of education are concerned with, the examination of the concepts of rights and equality. But they are not the kind of writing that would be likely to appear in a philosophical journal. They are not 'pure' analysis and reasoning. This is because my own practical experience has led me, while learning what I can from the philosophers of education, to take a view that includes what is (quite properly from their point of view) not their immediate concern. My work with Unesco and in Commonwealth education, for instance, has led me to reflect not only on the meaning of the term 'rights' in education but on the significance of the fact that it is now being everywhere invoked. That, through discussion with friends in such work, has led me to the view of rights as 'emergent' in terms of practicability, a point that I do not recall having come across in writing on the subject by any philosopher. Again, in my chapter on Equality I have been very much concerned with the expression of my own values in this matter (a philosopher either would not be or would not allow this to come so much to the fore). I have thus drawn on the philosophy of education, but have not written 'philosophy'. I have been concerned with something broader. It may have been done well or ill. But what I am concerned to maintain is that there is a place for this kind of contribution even though some philosophers might feel that it was not abstract enough, was too pragmatic, or relied too much on commonsense. I would not take that view.

The specialised study of the philosophy of education needs no defence, and it is quite properly a severe and in some sense an abstract discipline. But the question does arise as to how far it should restrict itself to what its practitioners believe to be its own sphere and its own code of discourse. In a recent BBC programme, for instance, Professor Gilbert Ryle was asked how he could have given so much attention to 'perception' without considering at all the considerable volume of work by psychologists and physiologists as to how we do perceive. He replied that he was concerned with a different sort of question. As a lay listener I was disposed to concede this up to a point, but I was not quite convinced. On a matter where several disciplines have something to contribute is it quite right for one of them to ignore the others?

It would be foolish to be dogmatic about this. But there is a natural professional tendency for groups to form, to develop their special terminology (which may short-circuit perpetual explanations since the code is understood within the professional group) and to become a little more exclusive than is good for mental health. I remember hearing about a meeting of philosophers of education to discuss the philosophy of art. I asked which artists had been invited to join them. 'Oh, none,' I was told. 'They wouldn't understand what we were talking about.' Good heavens! I thought. How far can spinning your coterie cocoons go? Of course the philosophers might on occasions have had to explain themselves to non-philosophers, and that might have been within limits a salutary thing. But there always have been, and still are, artists who are quite articulate in words and have said important things about what happens when they express themselves in their medium – to say nothing of artists in words themselves, like poets. Nor, I gathered, were even art or music critics to share in these deliberations. I cannot help feeling that art and literary criticism that does not keep close to actual pictures or music or creative writing will lack reality (that was what was wrong with Professor Hirst's paper 'The Fine Arts as a Unique Form of Knowledge'). There is a necessary abstraction in every kind of philosophical study, but it seems to me that philosophers of education should always have present somewhere in their minds real schools, real teachers and parents, and real children.

Much as we owe to the remarkable development of the philosophy of education in recent years I think it is cultivating a distinctive style that has its dangers. An elaboration of the abstract when speaking of a rich context can be sterile. As Professor Atkinson, himself a professor of philosophy, says in commenting on two contributors to the *Philosophers Discuss Education* symposium, their failure fairly to confront each other resulted partly from 'their attempting to discuss what are at bottom matters of educational policy in excessively abstract terms'.

The second kind of educational thinking that I would like to consider I have called pedagogical. This is a slightly awkward word. The abstract noun 'pedagogics' is not assimilated into English and before now I have protested at international conferences that it should not be used to translate the apparently wider German and French equivalents. The German *pädagogik* almost means 'education', though not 'upbringing'. The Unesco *Institut für Pädagogik* in Hamburg is so called, though the English title is the Unesco Institute for Education. Its publication, the *International Review of Education*, is called *La Revue Internationale de Pédagogie* in French. Again, in English the term 'pedagogue' is, like 'pedant', one of abuse. 'Pedogogical', however, though we do not use it much, is free from obloquy and is useful to describe the teacher's concern with what he teaches and the methods he uses in doing so. That is what I mean by it here.

Now, as we have seen, some of the teacher's thinking about what he does may be called philosophical. For the sake not merely of theoretical interest but of practical behaviour he must think what he means by words like 'authoritarian' and 'permissive'. He must ask whether he thinks of punishment as mainly retributive or reformative or just protective of the school society so that it can get on with its work; otherwise he will surely do something unconsidered that afterwards he will feel was not right.

Again, some of his thinking will be sociological. He must consider what sort of a social community his school is, and what it might be. He must know something of the social background from which his pupils come into school every day. And he will probably give some thought to the role of education in society and the part the school can play in society. But all this is thinking about education in the broad sense. Most of the time his professional thinking is about what he should teach and how he should teach it.

How far can we describe such thinking as theoretical? Insofar as it is, it is perceptibly nearer to what Professor Hirst calls working theory than the other kinds of theory I have mentioned. Some of it must derive from study of the ways in which children develop, both affectively and cognitively; and this now does form a fairly coherent body of theory. This body of theory, like its analogues in the pre-clinical studies in medicine, is too important to be picked up as he goes along and is studied by the teacher in its own right in his initial training if only so that he can draw on a repertoire of knowledge and understanding when a practical problem arises.

This is not to imply that our present knowledge of child psychology is as sure a guide as the knowledge available to a doctor when he wants to know which bone has been broken and how it should articulate with others, or whether a patient has this disease or that – and even there diagnosis may go wrong. But no one can deny that we have a better understanding now than fifty years ago as to how children develop. Perhaps as important, we have formed the habit of asking the right questions: for instance, that if a child is not learning well the explanation may be, not laziness or ill-will, but something to do with his present stage of development or his individual psychological make-up. In other words, the teacher can draw on a body of tested, if not unequivocal, experience that gives him a conceptual framework for his daily work in class or school.

Failure to understand what working pedagogical theory is has led to much foolish criticism of what is done in departments and colleges of education. (I am not saying that some of it is not dull. I have met people, often from the United States, who have wanted to train as teachers but who have lost patience with the dreary 'theory' in their courses. What was wrong was not that there was theory, but that it was not shown to be in vital contact with reality and that as presented it was too often just plain boring.)

Why not, say some critics, drop all this theory and train teachers practically? Why not, for instance, really train them to teach children how to read? Well, if a child is backward in reading there are many possible explanations. For one thing it is useful to understand that mere forwardness at an early age, or its reverse, does not appear to be of great significance. Reading seems to come to some children early. Others, who will become perfectly competent readers, may not be reading until a year or more later. But suppose the case is more serious. Leaving out things that apply to every child learning to read English, such as the difficulty occasioned by the irregularity of our traditional orthography (which learning through i.t.a. can correct), for a particular child the trouble may be physical, poor hearing or poor eyesight or slight brain damage. It may be associated with general very poor intelligence. It may be connected with the fact that its mother did not 'talk' to it when it was still incapable of speech. There may be emotional disturbances which set up a blockage. Now if you have gone into the research and the reasoning from it on these varied but related matters, you get a framework of ideas for dealing with cases of difficulty in practice. You have something like a working theoretical equipment. This is what 'theory' is in relation to reading. What a different picture this gives from the simple notion that all a teacher has to do is to teach Johnny his letters! And if there is no difficulty of any of these kinds, there is still a question of the best method, or combination of methods, for teaching people how to read. How far is 'look and say' a good method, or how far are children purporting to be taught in this way in actual fact using a measure of 'phonic' analysis, as some research has suggested? You just can't scrap 'theory' and be competent as a teacher of reading at all.

To give teachers routine training, instead of genuine professional education, is now out of the question. For one thing, there is not a subject taught where methods of teaching are not matters of dispute. The teacher has to think for himself and make up his own mind. Is he for the new mathematics or not? Does he sympathise with the new emphasis on lively speech in early English teaching as distinct from emphasis on grammar and spelling? In the introduction to the sciences how far is he willing to press discovery methods? In the teaching of modern languages does he welcome the new stress on speech and learning actual speech patterns as distinct from memorising tables of conjugations and declensions and trusting that the learner will be able to apply them in real situations?

One reason for his having to make up his own mind is that there is no invariable best method. Some methods in general may clearly be better than others, but some methods are better suited to some children than others and some better suited to one teacher's personal style than others. I would even say that one might learn better under a teacher who was by temperament clearly directive, even authoritarian, and whose methods went with his strength, than from someone of that temperament who had been persuaded into a 'democratic' style he did not really believe in.

This need for variety and flexibility is something that headteachers and administrators surely must understand. Pedagogical theory has little chance of being fruitful if the framework of organisation in the school or the school system is unsympathetic. There must be a degree of order in things, but this is to help the teacher, and through the teacher the children, not to frustrate what is creative in their work.

Yet if the administrator does not always understand this, it is no less true that the teacher does not always understand the thinking, and the very necessary thinking, of the administrator. Let us now turn to this third kind of thinking about education.

Administration is a means, not an end. The end of educational administration is better education. It follows that when an educational administrator thinks about administration he should not think of it for its own sake, but as promoting better education. If he does not think about education himself then he should subordinate what he does to the demands set by those who do. Unfortunately these apparently innocent observations raise a number of difficulties.

Some people undoubtedly have a gift for organisation. Others, however gifted, are hopeless at it. A good administrator by temperament may go a long way without any real technical knowledge of the field in which he is operating. His is the outside eye when the technical experts are pressing their particular points of view and are too deep in the wood to see anything but their favourite trees. It is not difficult to make a list of the things that any administrator will want and seek to get, whatever his field of operation: clear formulation of aims, reasonable differentiation of function among those involved in the work, a clear chain of command, a proper phasing of successive steps in a programme so that if step four depends on step three step three is completed first, and perhaps above all a practical relationship between what is aimed at and the available resources. If he is wise he will also insist on fall-back plans, things to do if something goes wrong with the execution of the plan. Well, if this list conveys the things that an administrator must insist on, is it not very general, applicable to a business, or a hospital, or a school-system? Should we not be justified in appointing to educational administration someone who had shown in some quite different kind of work that his administrative thinking and practice were sound?

One obvious danger in doing that is that we may encourage the idea that administration is an end in itself and the fact that its field of operation at the moment is education is purely incidental.

It is certainly possible for someone who has thought about education and is seriously interested in it, even though he has not come up through the educational system, so to 'identify' with the purposes of education as to be a good educational administrator. But this is not as common as British civil service practice tends to assume. Administrative requirements tend to be fairly clear-cut. Educational values are often subtle. The surface arguments are commonly in favour of the former and the damage that can be done is less measurable, as we saw in the case of 'payment by results'. This is the kind of grudge the educationist very often has against the administrator who does not have good educational values uppermost in his mind.

Though this is true, the individual teacher and research worker must understand the kind of thinking an educational administrator does. It is less 'pure' than that of the philosopher, more concerned with large-scale material factors and less with individuals than the teacher's. It is to a high degree contingent thinking, contingent on what is laid down politically, on what is physically and financially possible, on what can be done with available human resources. A marvellously creative teacher or a most penetrating and subtle philosopher may be a hopeless muddler administratively. The administrator must try to persuade him, for after all education is the end and administration the means, but he must make some effort to understand the administrator, for without not only a good system but one that will accommodate his creative waywardness he could not do his work. In fact most teachers and academics will see the administrator's point if it is put to them fairly and they have no reason to feel that they are being pushed around.

In general it is more likely to be the administrator, especially if he has come from some other kind of administration and does not have education in his bones, who is less likely to understand the values and the needs of the teacher and the academic. Some succeed, remarkably. The feeling that ultimately they exercise the power (even though indirectly) is often not good for them. They may well feel that teachers and educationists do not have a grasp of national problems, and this, together with the feeling that after all they are persons of integrity trying to satisfy ministers, Parliament, the press and the public as well as the teachers (to say nothing of the Treasury) all at the same time, makes it a great temptation to them to constitute themselves into a court that decides after hearings but not a conference that works to a consensus.

Administrative thinking in education, like the two other kinds we have discussed, is distinctive and indispensable, but by itself not enough. The philosopher, the teacher, the administrator who see this have the kind of balance that, we say, shows their commonsense.

Chapter 10

The Concept of Research in Education

In some places there is impatience with educational research. In others there is almost a mystique about it. As our last essay in commonsense, can we look at this concept and see what the place of research is in relation to other kinds of writing about education?

I would like to distinguish between three kinds of writing about education: what I would call research proper, writing that illuminates through personal experience, and policy papers. But what, it may be asked, is meant by research proper?

The word 'research' is confusingly used in English. We speak of a first degree (and sometimes a second) that is based on course work, and distinguish it from a research degree that is awarded on the basis of some special study. But not all such studies are scientific. They may be philosophical or concerned with literature and the arts. To describe these as research helps the non-scientific subjects to fit into the academic scheme of things that has developed in this country first under the influence of Germany and then of the United States; in particular it seems to legitimise appeals for funds for such studies. But it has one serious disadvantage. With us the word 'research' has a strong pull in the direction of methods appropriate to the natural sciences, and this may lead to falsification of the nature of other studies.

This has often been sadly so in literature, especially in the United States. When I have my own last *viva* at the Day of Judgement I hope I may be given a little credit for trying to persuade one graduate student that the way to study colour in the poetry of Keats was not to count the number of times he used the names of the seven colours of the spectrum. The dean of the School of English in an American university once said to me that he could not get funds to extend the faculty library but that if he had the nerve to say he was founding an Institute of Bibliotherapy (which only means making yourself better by reading books) he would no doubt be successful. Such stories (and they are endless) would be amusing if they were not so sad. 'Dress it up as science' has too often been the disastrous maxim of research studies in the humanities. And education is no less a humane study than a scientific one. Better one sensitive and personal study of something important, however often it has been 'done' before, than additions to knowledge, as it is called, about things that are of no serious critical interest, or at least not enough to justify the sacrifice of three of the best years of a young student's life. The first question to be asked of a proposed investigation is: is it significant and therefore worthwhile? The second is: are the methods you propose to employ appropriate to it?

Where it is proposed that the methods should be scientific, and the answer to these two questions is yes, the insistence on that favourite word of education research workers, rigorous, is entirely right. Unless such research is rigorous it is of very little value (though, as I shall explain, by rigorous I mean not necessarily completely so, but as much as the circumstances make possible). This means that influences must be excluded that distort true findings, such as the use of inadequate or non-representative samples in a survey, the failure to compare like with like or to isolate the features that are being compared, or the intrusion of undisclosed value-judgements. Such research is what I would call research proper. And on the whole I am in favour of using the word research strictly, to refer to studies that are appropriate to such broadly scientific methods and that fail if they are not as rigorous as they can possibly be made.

Unfortunately people often ask for research where the questions they want answered are not really research questions. A proposal once came to my desk, as I understood it inviting research into the best form of the 'act of worship' ordained for publicly owned schools by the Education Act of 1944. A colleague I consulted who likes these acts of worship (I do not) agreed with me that this was not a research question. It depended on what was meant by 'best'. Until that was settled, at least for the purposes of this research, research could not take place.

The narrowness of the implications of our word 'research' may be felt by comparison with the French. We could not translate the title of Proust's novel as 'Research into Lost Time'. When the French refer to what we should call simply 'research' they have to specify what kind of research it is, and say *recherches scientifiques*. We have the same narrowness in the word 'science'. French 'science', though it has a narrower sense, like German *Wissenschaft* can refer to any systematically ordered knowledge or study. Theology may have been called the Queen of the Sciences at the University of Paris, but it sounds very odd in English because of the more limited scope we have come to give the word 'science'. (I refer of course to the terminology, not to the acceptability or otherwise of the claim.) I doubt if we can escape from these usages now. I would prefer to say that humane studies are just as important as scientific ones, but since they are not either science or research as we normally use those terms, to call them studies. This, it seems to me, is the only way to avoid pulling them in a wrong direction. They should have their recognised autonomy.

Education is a mixed field of study. It is when we are in the realm of facts rather than values that the term research is appropriate. I hope I shall not be accused of naïve empiricism if I make this distinction (I shall return to it later). Our value-systems no doubt influence our decision to examine certain facts rather than others and to some extent govern our percepts and our concepts, but there is still a distinction valid at a practical level between establishing what the position is now in any given social matter and saying what we think it ought to be. Finding out the facts might often seem to call for the discriminating pertinacity of an administrative rather than a scientific kind. Nevertheless appearances may be deceptive and in at least two respects such inquiries have a strong analogy with the proceedings of science. Techniques (logical or statistical) for isolating the facts one wants to study are akin to the abstraction from the confused impurities of the daily world that the laboratory affords to the scientist. And secondly the research worker purports to show facts uncoloured by prejudice, taste or personal preference and therefore must aim at the kind of objectivity, testable by public methods, that is cardinal in scientific research. To take a simple example. If we wish to compare the educational development of two countries we need to know such things as the proportion of each age-group that does not go to school and the tendencies up or down over a period of time, and the percentage of those in primary school who go on to the secondary school. But the mere percentage of those in the primary school who go on tells us little unless we know the percentage of the age-group in the primary school. And what does the term primary school cover, a schooling of four years, or six, or something else? And are we speaking of the entry to or the completion of primary school education? Are we comparing like with like in the two countries? And it goes without saying that such inquiries must not be coloured by prejudice or initial subjective impression: that Scottish education is better than English (or vice versa) or that China is on the right road and Brazil on the wrong (or vice versa). In all this the statement that research is concerned with the facts and should not be influenced by value-judgements is intelligible and useful.

However, we think of typical scientific research as based on experiment, and this is where the great difficulty of educational research lies. In a laboratory you can abstract from ordinary life. You have the pre-conditions necessary for being rigorous. In educational research, as in the social sciences, the great difficulty is to control situations so as to give you as nearly as possible the laboratory situation although you are working in the field with teachers, children, parents, administrators and schools, all individually different and none of them neatly measurable. The dilemma is that if we refuse to investigate except in near-perfect conditions we ignore most of the important educational problems, whereas if we try to tackle them we are bound to be less than completely rigorous. You can be aware of the dangers and try to guard against them. You can employ ingenious statistical techniques to separate out what you want to get at from intrusive alien matters. But you are not in a laboratory. When Dr John Downing was conducting his work at the London Institute to see whether children could learn to read better with i.t.a. than with the ordinary alphabet he well understood that he could not be completely rigorous and that his research might invite purist criticism. When you are working in the field, not the laboratory, your obligation is to be as rigorous as the situation will permit. You are a scientist working in a non-scientific situation. But you are still concerned with publicly verifiable data and you are testing hypotheses, making your work as free of subjective judgements as you can.

In this kind of situation (a normal one in educational research) proof is a little more problematical than in laboratory science. It is bound to be; and the reply to impatient public bodies that ask for a straight answer to what they think is a straight question is that one can only accumulate and continue to test the evidence and come to an increasingly firm conviction that something is so or not. Educational research may often give us enough to go on. Whether the percentage of children, judged by their subsequent careers, who would seem to have been placed on the wrong side of the '11 plus', is ten or twenty matters much less than the fact that the number has been substantial. However, the fact that much educational research is of this not quite determinate kind* makes me suspect those who use the word 'findings' as if they were saying 'Holy Writ'. This, of course, is being the reverse of scientific. One is especially sceptical about this kind of confidence when such 'findings' run counter to most widely attested and on the face of it convincingly interpreted experience.

A good example is the question of the size of classes. I heard a distinguished educational psychologist at an international conference blandly assert that there was no research evidence to support the idea that children learn better in small classes than in large ones. He obviously thought that this settled the matter. And this has been resoundingly said time and time again now until influential fund-granting institutions like the World Bank seem uncritically to accept it. Ordinary working teachers will have none of it. They are quite capable of understanding that the question is not what will make their daily task more tolerable but which regime enables children to learn better; and you cannot persuade them that large classes are as good as small, just like that. Are they flat-earthers? Or are the people who quote these research findings wrong somewhere? This is a very serious question, for it guides policy where resources are scarce. A reduction in the size of classes means more teachers, and teachers' salaries are by far the largest item in the annual budget of schools.

I will return later to the need for research workers to understand the political context in which their findings may be discussed and misinterpreted, but apart from this there are one or two obvious things to say. The first (and this was pointed out to me by a research colleague) is that one must know the limits within which the research has made its findings and not extrapolate heedlessly. There are teaching procedures where increasing the size of the group may not matter much. If you are lecturing to 200 people you might as well lecture to 300. Similarly, the difference between a class of thirty and thirty-five may not be of all that moment. Indeed, if in a larger class the teacher feels he must concentrate on a few specified skills (reading ability, for instance) and not allow expansive roving into other

---

* The latest warning that such findings are not Holy Writ is noted in the newspapers as I write. An inquiry in 1972 – which led to the setting up of the Bullock Committee – said that the progress in reading standards evident up to 1964 had more recently been curtailed and that illiteracy was on the increase. A new inquiry says the suggestion that there has been a fall in reading standards is not right and points out what was wrong with the 1972 work. Both reports have come from the National Foundation for Educational Research. Even the most careful body in educational research can need to correct itself!

things in which the children may be interested, you may actually get better results, when you test for those skills alone, in the larger than in the smaller class. But the important point is that the difference between a class of thirty or more and a class of fifteen is quite another matter. This, in rough terms, is the difference in size of classes between the publicly maintained and the private schools, and this is a point that weighs heavily with parents concerned with educational as distinct from merely social advantages in sending their children (if they can afford it) to private schools. Are they flying in the face of research? I do not think so, and know of no parent who has made a decision on these grounds who thinks he is.

We are told these days that we must get as close to individualised learning as we can, and rightly so. Children are different, needing to go at different speeds, interested in and capable of different things. The more children you have in your care the harder it must be to give individual attention to the children who need it, when they need it. Indeed the harder it is to know them as persons. Is there a catch somewhere in this rather obvious reasoning, which research has now revealed? I find it hard to believe.

We are also told increasingly to think of the curriculum as all that is learned in a school. Certainly extrapolation from tests in, say, reading and arithmetic, even if these could not be faulted, would be rash if covering the total learning experience of school. I would like to hear the comment of the educational psychologist to whom I have referred (and of another who was equally confident in print about this) on the experience described by the writer who calls herself Miss Read in her novel *Fresh from the Country*.[1] It describes how a country girl comes to teach at Elm Hill, a school in greater London. This school, we are told, had been built for 350 children but within eighteen months was housing 500. The ten classrooms which were to have held thirty children apiece were now a tight mass of desks, wedged so closely together that it was difficult to move up and down the meagre gangways left between the rows. The numbers were nearer fifty than forty in each class, and the spacious hall which had so delighted the new headmistress and her staff now housed two more classes. And so on.

In Chapter Seven (entitled 'Occupational Hazards') the effect of this on the work of the new teacher is described. 'The one great, glaring, wicked problem to Anna was the size of her class. Fond of them as she was as individuals, collectively they constituted an unwieldly, noisy, and exhausting mass.' Getting them (forty-eight of them) along a corridor was a daunting task. 'It was impossible to watch them all, and one high-spirited push would do much damage, and one boy was lame, with his leg in irons.' The classroom was far too full.

To Anna, who had been trained to allow freedom of movement and a certain amount of talking in the classroom, the conditions were doubly frustrating. She found herself bound to quell quite legitimate noise for the simple reason that she was trying to deal with twice its normal volume, and the free traffic of children from their desks to the shelves and cupboards to fetch their own working materials had to be severely restricted. . . . It perturbed her to think how little time she could conscientiously give to each child. She liked to mark all written work with the child beside her, but soon found that this was impossible to do every time with over forty children. She set herself to hear each child read at least twice a week, and knew in her heart that it should be a daily exercise if conditions would allow.

And so it goes on, with accents of truth that every such beleagured teacher will recognise as true. I decline to believe that a few pieces of limited research conducted in the United States invalidate it. Those who trust such research and allow extrapolation to popular phrases like 'It has been shown by research that large classes are as good as small ones' seem to me to be doing a great disservice to education (that is to say, to children) and not least to the standing in the eyes of teachers and parents of educational research. If they had to choose between sending their children to such a school as the one described here and a reasonably good private school with no more than fifteen in a class, I know which they would choose. This is an example of overconfidence in extrapolatory potential not unconnected with the prestige of scientific research, and would be so even on the assumption (which only someone more expert than I could challenge or support) that within their specified original limits the experiments concerned were scientifically valid enough. A second distortion is that of using methods that may look scientific when apparently less scientific ones would be more appropriate. I recall a quite costly investigation into the school-system of an American city designed to examine what officials should do if they wished to improve the curricula in the schools. The conclusion seemed to be that they should try to carry the teachers, the public and the students along with them. Well, of course. Does one need research to tell one that? And it was all written up in what to an English ear often seemed to be jargon. What might have been illuminating was something quite different: a sensitive analysis of attempted reforms that had gone right or gone wrong with an effort to bring out what were predominant in each case. But this would have been, unfortunately, much less professional. As it stood the report seemed to me to give arguments to those who ask why we need research to tell us what we know perfectly well without it.

That question, however, is not as simple as it might appear. On the one hand there have been examples of the erection of scaffolding to build mousetraps, and I have just given one. But on the other hand a piece of research that leads to no conclusion that we do not hold already, but shows how and why it is so, can be valuable. Even the experiments in class size to which I have referred may be held to have contributed something to our growing realisation that a single standardised grouping for every learning purpose does not have much to commend it. The optimum size varies with what is being learned and the procedures for teaching and learning it. A teacher needs to be sensitive to the differences in situations: when a child or a student should try to get hold of something by himself, when the interactions in a small group may promote learning, and when the economies of large groups are perfectly in place. And without a great number of research studies into these different situations, and rigour not only in their conduct but in the deductions made from them, it will not be possible to build up a general understanding that can be communicated to the future teacher in his initial training and be present in his mind to be matched against his own professional experience. This is one answer to critics who might say that there are too many graduate students now doing educational research. Given sensible selection of topics of inquiry and a proper relation of methods to aims this is indeed not so.

When I come on to speak of policy papers I shall emphasise the need for much more research than we usually have for our policy statements. But leaving that on one side for the moment, think what our understanding of what we are doing would be were it not for the educational research of, above all, the present century. We do have a considerably better understanding of the way in which children develop, cognitively and affectively, than we did, and our education has taken increasing account of this. We can identify much more surely than we did the extent, incidence and nature of inequalities in education. We understand much better than formerly the significance of the social setting of our schools and of homes and neighbourhoods for particular children's education. We do realise that methods of teaching ought not to be dependent on rule of thumb but the subject of rational inquiry and testing. We have some research that has had its effect, as in the case of selection at 11 to which I have referred. We have some research that has been published for all to see (such as the investigation into i.t.a to which I have also referred) that most authorities and teachers continue to ignore. Our whole way of thinking about what we are doing in education has been decisively modified by the work of a long line of eminent research workers from Sir Cyril Burt to Piaget, Philip Vernon, Bernstein and many others in many countries. So I would not have my criticisms of what educational research sometimes becomes through misunderstanding of its nature as in any way a suggestion that we have too much of it. We emphatically do not have enough. Official support of the National Foundation for Educational Research and of research posts, right up to research chairs, has been far too niggardly in this country. And merely commissioned research is not enough: how could Piaget have done his work had he had to wait upon the discovery by the city of Geneva that it wanted quick answers to immediate practical questions? But I do insist that research is not the only way by which we can arrive at a better understanding of education.

There is of course, if one confines the term educational research to the area where the scientific analogy is broadly acceptable, the whole effort to understand through analytical reflection on our experience. This is broadly what philosophy of education is concerned with. I have never been at ease with the ascription to it of the word research, but of its cardinal importance there can be no doubt; and I shall not labour the point. The historical dimension is also indispensable in the study of education, and here the word research is more appropriate. Yet it is also true to say that the distorting effect of the analogy with the sciences can at times be seen here. While it is indeed arguable that one cannot be a historian without the experience of contact with primary sources, the tendency to under-rate work that offers a wider understanding, and is therefore inevitably based in large part on secondary sources, has gone too far. What is all this detailed discovery of minor facts for if not to contribute to a better-informed general view? Having referred briefly to these studies that often pass under the name of research but that I would prefer to describe simply as studies, and noting that no one is likely to dispute their importance whatever name is given to them, I would like to pass on to the second kind of writing about education that I said at the outset was valuable, and that is so different from anything that could be called research that the very difference may help to show what research is and is not.

Some of the writing about education that is most worth reading is the expression of personal or imaginative experience. Some of this writing has a research element in it, though it could not be described as research in the sense in which I have been using the word. There may have been some seeking out of facts, some investigation of situations, something perhaps of social or historical research in the broad sense, but the purpose is not to establish objective generalisations so much as to illuminate through a felt experience. Such a book was Richard Hoggart's *Uses of Literacy*,[2] which so movingly evoked the working-class culture of a generation ago in the industrial north. (The title of the French translation, incidentally, was *La Culture des Pauvres*.) Such, with perhaps rather more research in them, were the books of Jackson and Marsden on much the same theme.[3]

Even more powerful in their effects, perhaps, have been the innumerable pictures, in autobiographies and in purely imaginative literature, of schools and schoolmasters, teachers and students. Perhaps the most quoted phrase of all about the sense of vocation of the scholar-teacher is Chaucer's, from his picture of the Clerk of Oxenford, 'And gladly wolde he lerne, and gladly teche'. What an effect that one line has had over the centuries! If you wish really to feel what it is like to be forever shut out from the education that in your heart you know is yours by right, read of Hardy's Jude the Obscure, shut out from the Oxford colleges that he passed by every day. If you want to feel what it is like to stand, just down from college, in front of your first difficult class, the famous chapter by D. H. Lawrence in *The Rainbow* will bring it home to you as no statistics will. I have already mentioned one book by 'Miss Read', the author of *Village School*. There is no need to multiply examples. While such writing is not altogether ignored in the preparation of our teachers it is normally regarded as a kind of secondary, almost leisure-time extra; and this, I am sure, is mistaken. Such imaginative writing makes learning and teaching a living experience. The preparation of teachers is a poor thing if it does not tap these sources, for they transform teaching from a task to an imaginatively enriched life.

This kind of imaginative understanding is especially important for those who are going to teach children in a culture or a sub-culture different from that in which they have been brought up. It is sometimes said that most of our teachers have middle-class values and manners and fail when they try to impose these on working-class children. This debate has been considerably muddle-headed. One would almost suppose from some of the critics that it is wrong to open the possibilities for working-class children of planning for the future as well as living for today and of enjoyment of our great writers, for these are, somehow, middle-class things. This is nonsense. But it is true that in manners (including manners of speech) a girl from a grammar school of good suburban tone may find herself unimaginatively out of sympathy with the youngsters out of, say, the background that Richard Hoggart describes. A colleague of mine at the Canberra College of Education, an anthropologist by training, got his student teachers to go into the sub-cultures of the young people of that presumably rather select city; and they were amazed to find that such diversity existed, and I do not doubt became better and more understanding teachers because of the experience.

This kind of imaginative leap, based indeed on knowledge but given life by the imagination, is even more important when the difference is not one merely of sub-cultures, but of cultures, as it is with teachers who are going from an advanced country to teach in the schools of the Third World. To illustrate this, and some of the difficulties involved, I would like to refer in a little detail to a book that I read when I was professor of education in what is now called the Department of Education in Developing Countries in the London Institute; and for two reasons. The first is that my story illustrates the tendency to under-rate imaginative literature of which I have complained. The book was not in our departmental library, and when I asked why I was told that the reason had been that it was not scientific, not real anthropology. I asked for it to be put in. The second reason is that this book raises the question whether studies that give real insight into another culture can be strictly scientific, in the sense of value-free.

The book, called *Return to Laughter*, was written by an American woman anthropologist who used a pseudonym, Elinore Smith Bowen. One hopes that she did not do this for fear that her standing as an anthropologist would be diminished if it were known that she had written such a book at all. But it looks as if this was the reason. She vouches for the soundness of the anthropological setting she describes and for the fact that the people in the book were such as she had met in the course of her work in Africa. But the story was of course 'made up', and she wished to keep such a kind of writing distinct from her scientific anthropological studies. One can accept this as proper enough, but it was validly complementary to those and it is a pity she felt she had somehow to go into disguise. It was, in the sense I have described, an imaginary account of what it was like for a Western woman to try to live as a member of an African tribe, and I should consider such a book well worth reading for anyone who was going to teach in a pre-technical society.

The book dates from the last years of colonial administration (it was published, by Gollancz, in 1954) and she went to live with the tribe with the slightly hesitant blessing of the district officer. He held the chief responsible for her, and to make this easier for him the chief after an awkward interlude got her moved into his own compound, living with his womenfolk. But she found in this situation that she had no access to the men's deliberations and indeed to a whole range of activities that she wanted to study. Things came to a head at a wedding. One of the women said to her clearly that she must choose: if she wanted to be treated as a distinguished visitor that would be all right, the bride could be brought out to see her, and she could ask any questions she desired. Or she could be for the time one of them, dance as they did and in short do what they did. She chose the latter – and gallantly tried to fall in line and dance in their way with them.

But worse was to come. A woman of the tribe she liked was in obvious danger of dying in child-birth. Something was going badly wrong. The tribe had its own way of dealing with such dangers, magical, unscientific ways, as the anthropologist (now turned all Western) knew them to be. She begged to be allowed to get the woman to her car, left some way along the trail, and get her skilled help. But no, they believed in their magic, not hers, and she was living as one of them. The woman died. It was a story, though how far in this particular founded on fact one does not know. But it raises, and validly, a very important point. How far can you be just a scientific and detached research worker if you wish to understand and convey what it feels like to be a woman in such a tribe? If you do become sympathetically involved, are not value-judgements bound to come in? It is an old question in social studies, rarely so poignantly illustrated as here.

Although one must be honest with the facts and as free from prejudice as one possibly can, yet educational or other social studies cannot be just written off because the author clearly has his values and the judgements following from them. Professor Gunnar Myrdal in his book *Value in Social Theory*[4] challenges much of the conventional wisdom on this point, and his editor, Paul Streeten, refers in his Introduction to Hume's famous complaint that writers on morality invariably start by describing what is and then move imperceptibly, and without warning the reader, to what they think ought to be, as if the latter followed from the former, though they do not explain how it does. Mr Streeten does not say that Professor Myrdal would suggest that this does not matter, but he does say that Myrdal has seen that the business is much more complicated, that the values enter into the work of a students society as essential principles, forming the structure of theoretical thought, giving it meaning and direction. It is not even enough to make the value-judgements explicit: they permeate such work through and through.

The apparent difficulty here is that we may be arguing at two different levels. It is obviously true that nearly all the most influential writing on educational and social matters has come from writers with a strong sense of values, and mere objectivity would not have given them the insight they show because of their value-laden drives. What Myrdal insists on – and up to this point I agree – is that values should be made explicit. But beyond this I think that what he says is true only at one level, perhaps the most important but certainly not the most immediate. His truth, that our very percepts and concepts as well as the direction of our minds towards the facts we think most significant are associated with and to some extent dependent on our values, can become a very dangerous one if it leads people to suppose that at the working level objectivity in the examination of evidence is not of quite paramount importance. At this level it is still true in a sense we all understand that 'is' and 'ought' are not to be confused. In getting at the facts of a situation the research worker must be concerned with what is. In policy formulations we are, quite obviously, concerned also with what we think ought to be, though the facts must be got right. The old-fashioned scientific positivism of people like Durkheim, that policy could be scientifically deduced from social facts, just is not so. It may be a fact that people hold certain values, but a value is not the same thing as a fact; it is a preference. Otherwise social studies are nothing more than market research: the best product is the one most people buy. The whole debate as to whether what we do want is what we should want, which is the essence of moral development, is ruled out. While one can accept Myrdal's protest that it is naïve to make Hume's distinction into a sufficient psychological or philosophical explanation of the relationship of values to facts, at the commonsense working level it is still true, and very importantly true, that the research worker asked to report on the facts should do so, and with the greatest effort to keep out distortion and personal or social bias; and that the policy maker who is concerned with making things better, with what ought to be, should not only have an explicit concern with values but should get his facts right.

The third kind of writing about education that I would like to consider is precisely this. It is what I have called the policy paper. This covers many formally different kinds of document but draws attention to what they have in common. Such papers have to be within the limits of what is practicable. They should draw upon all available relevant research. And they should be inspired by considered, explained and defended values.

There is a strong and good tradition in this country, dating back at least to the middle years of last century, that public commissions charged with reporting should investigate; and the sheer weight of evidence collected has often shocked public opinion so that action has followed. This is not quite the same thing as research, in the sense in which I have been using the term in this paper. It is the assembling of facts, but not also the skilled treatment of them (for instance by statistical methods) to bring out what might not be quite apparent on the surface. Among our more recent educational reports perhaps the Crowther Report[5] might be credited with beginning the now-established tradition of researches for the purpose of its policy recommendations. It did not do this for the whole of its work (its assumptions about the interests of young adults in the sixth form are mostly folklore) but it did, for instance, utilise figures from the last year of compulsory service to show how many of our abler children had left school at the age of 15. More conspicuously, it was the Robbins Committee[6] that set in train a whole series of investigations to provide it with data that it needed and that until then were not there. The collection and processing of educational data should be a continuous function, especially of the Department of Education and Science, and the relevant facts and figures should mostly be available when a Committee meets and has to report against time. In this country in recent years we have improved very much in this respect.

Such a data bank, however, is unlikely to be a substitute for some specific research demanded by certain policy inquiries. When Mr Short, as Minister of Education, asked the institutes of education to report on their work and their structure we realised in the London Institute that there was one basic question that for lack of evidence we were not in a position to answer. We trained teachers. Yes; but for what? What in reality did a new teacher do when he or she first joined a school? How was he expected, for instance, to divide his day between classroom teaching and other activities? How much time on average did he have for the preparation of each lesson? How much time was taken up by marking pupils' work? How much did he use audio-visual aids? What was consciously done by his school to induct him into its life? Did he have a lighter load than his colleagues at first, or was he given the most difficult class because no one else wanted it? About none of these things did we have the facts – though we may have had impressions. To bring them under one heading, the question we could not answer was: what is the job description of the job for which we are training? To get such a job description was important, for until we had it we could not distinguish between that part of the training that was best done in advance and that part that was best done on the job. With the co-operation of two education authorities, Southend-on-Sea and Slough, we mounted inquiries into these matters, for primary and secondary schools respectively, and we found out a lot! Our rather hurried studies (from which we could not generalise too much because they were of particular localities only) were followed soon afterwards by the NFER's *The Teacher's Day*.[7] You cannot formulate a rational policy for institutions that train teachers without information of this kind.

Our ignorance of the mental and social life of children in the countries of the Third World is still immense, and this is especially serious while a good number of their teachers still come from the advanced countries, and their still numerous expert advisers do. A colleague of mine was talking with me a few years ago just after he had been at a small meeting of teachers in a part of Papua New Guinea to discuss the relative virtues of the old and the new mathematics. He asked if any teacher present knew how the people of that part of the country counted. None did. It was just assumed that they counted as most of the world did. Well, they didn't; and this was rather important to know if you were introducing children to number. (I found a very interesting account of how people count in at least one part of Papua New Guinea in that now defunct children's periodical *The Eagle*.)

Western children have made a considerable acquaintance with number before they start school at all. In many pre-technical societies naturally this is not so. You rarely handle money, you don't have shops and can't play at them, and you probably do not need to count to any high level. I shall long remember the desperate attempts of an African colleague of mine, a professor of medicine, to ascertain from a village assembly in the hinterland of Liberia what their infant mortality rate was there. The conception of percentages was quite unknown to them. In the end my colleague had to fix his eye on one of the livelier members of the group and ask if he would have considered himself lucky if he had had ten children and five grew up to be young men or women or, if the number was less, that he had perhaps been bewitched. Even knowledge as to a child's age was doubtful then (that was twenty years ago and the introduction of a census has no doubt improved matters): if you were a doctor or a teacher you just looked at his teeth and guessed.

These are simple examples concerning factual information. We are in an even worse state about mental processes concerned with family and social ways and with concepts. For decades mission schools in Africa taught that polygamy was a sin and at home it was a sign of status and affluence. What a conflict to set up in a child's mind about his parents! The right answer is not always simply to accept a local concept. That might interfere with genuine education too. I was once asked to take part in a series of talks at the London School of Hygiene and Tropical Medicine. The man who had spoken before me, an anthropologist, had talked about witchcraft in Africa and had said it did not conflict with medical science but offered an explanation of things where medicine left off. He had told the story of the African who had said that he quite understood that his daughter had contracted malaria because she had been bitten by an anopheles mosquito. But who had made the mosquito land on her cheek? That was where the witchcraft had come in. I asked my medical student audience if they were content with that explanation. I am glad to say they were not. They thought there was still a good deal for education to do.

I hope these fairly obvious examples will show that before we can make educational policy, or indeed just teach, either in our own culture or in others, we badly need evidence gained through research.

When we have our research data and results they have to be related to policy and to the far from laboratory situations in which policies are made and have to be carried out. Here I think greater use might well be made of what I think the Americans first called the 'position paper'. This is not a research paper, though it calls on the attested evidence. It is not yet a statement of final policy. But it indicates the general lines of policy that the research evidence, our values and our scales of priorities, and the practical possibilities, seem to suggest. Sometimes such position papers stop short of actual policy recommendations but demonstrate the necessary conditions of any successful policy. A very good example is *The World Educational Crisis,* which the author, Dr Philip Coombs, called a systems analysis.[8] It was intended as a basic position paper for the international conference held at Williamsburg, Virginia, a few years ago; and it was a pity that so excellent a lead was not more seriously followed up by the conference itself. There was no new research special to the book, but a cogent analysis of all the major factors in the light of the idea that you must look at the 'system' as a whole because all the parts are interconnected. We need many more studies of this kind, whether the educational subject be large or small, by people who are both research-conscious and aware of the social, political and administrative setting of any consequent action. At the moment research results too often reach the public in a popular form, through the newspaper or radio and television, and the often innocent research worker is sometimes unaware of what is happening to his careful work in the popularisation that ensues. Or if he becomes aware he may well get angry. (I am not suggesting, of course, that the reports of research workers should not be available to the public. I am saying that research workers show themselves insensitive to, or unaware of, the differences between their professional world and that of administration, politics and popular disputation.)

The practical setting in which research results are to be considered outside the laboratory or the study are rightly very much in the minds of officials and elected persons; one might even add, the setting in which the research worker conducts his work, or proposes to do so. (I was once pressed by a colleague to remonstrate with an education authority that seemed unfriendly to having his research students in their schools, and when I took the matter up with the chief education officer and his chairman they told me stories of what some research students – all in the not-to-be-questioned name of research – had wanted to do in their schools; and 'Remember', said the chairman, 'I am an elected person and have to face my electors.' I agreed that if they would be more welcoming I would urge my colleagues to see that procedures were not followed that would cause justified alarm among parents.)

Here, however, I am concerned more with the promulgation of results. The research worker is trying to find out the truth about something, and his findings may be unpalatable to someone or some group. Nothing can justify hushing them up. The one concession I would make (in agreement with Dr Alan Little, formerly research officer to the Inner London Education Authority, who made this point on an Open University programme) is that in some cases you may be more effective if you put the responsible officials in possession of your findings than if you rush into print. But you must be sure that they are not just going to bury them! What I am saying, however, is that if the research worker does not wish to contribute to falsity he needs to be very much aware of the setting in which his statements will be received. It seems to me that he can no more shrug off responsibility for this than the scientist can for the effects on mankind of the results of his work.

Let me revert to the rather overconfident assertion that there is no research evidence to suggest that children learn worse in large classes than in small ones. Apart from the other doubts about this assertion there is a distorting effect when it is translated into political and administrative terms. When so translated, large classes will mean overcrowded classes. The research worker may not have said that a classroom meant to hold thirty-five children is just as good a place for learning if it has forty-five children in it. The politician and financial officials, worried by the bill for teachers' salaries, are almost bound to leap on to this piece of research 'evidence' and turn it into something the research worker will protest, too late, that he did not mean. If he does not wish to be misunderstood would it be too much to ask him to foresee the danger and say that if we believe young children should be reasonably free to move about they can do that less the more children there are in a given space, and that his research does not point to the merits of overcrowding?

While we ought to expect politicians and officials to pay attention to the results of research they cannot be expected to have specialised knowledge or skills. What happens to the work of educational psychologists on the way to the ministry or County Hall is sometimes odd. The classic case is that of the '11 plus'. Did reputable psychologists ever say that there was something called general intelligence that could be accurately measured and did not change throughout life? Or did the Ministry of Education get it all wrong? In any case, which educational psychologists said that there were three distinct kinds of children, that tests could tell you which kind any particular child belonged to, and that he could therefore be confidently placed, to society's and also to his own benefit, in the appropriate one of three distinct types of secondary school?

I think there has been a shift of emphasis among psychologists over the years. This has been prompted, of course, by some of their own number, such as Professor Philip Vernon. Yet there have been good psychologists all the time who have been saying that intelligence tests are useful guides but should not be treated as more than that. There has undoubtedly been a considerable degree of misunderstanding but I cannot help feeling that the research workers themselves might have done more to guard against it. It *is* their business if they are concerned in practice with what they have made their concern. Even the most sophisticated, professionally, can be amongst the most naïve in this way. The immensely respected name of Sir Cyril Burt,* as almost his last act, turned up among the writers of the Black Papers. Can he have thought for a moment of the company he was keeping? He was one of those who welcomed the original use of these tests as helping the innate quality of a child to be revealed whatever the handicaps of his origins and environment, in other words as helping forward the spread of educational opportunity.

The most recent *cause célèbre* (and although it began in the early seventies it has hardly died down yet) has been that of Professor Jensen. In the crude popular version Professor Jensen was held to have said that black Americans were inferior in intelligence to white Americans and that schooling should take account of these differences. Now Jensen is clearly a skilled and serious research worker and those who denounced him should have read him with reasonable care. The response was less often one of counter-criticism than of hysteria. Jensen has been submitted to the most intolerable

* While this book was in page-proof there was an attack not only on some statistical errors made by Burt but on his integrity. There was a long correspondence in the *Times*, decisively dealt with by Professor Jensen. I see no reason to change my text.

intolerance, and often by people who call themselves liberals. I would stand up for Jensen against this sort of thing. Yet I have an uncomfortable feeling that at least in some degree, to use colloquial language, he asked for it. He wasn't sensitive to the setting in which his comments would be understood once they got outside the merely professional circle.

What Professor Jensen claimed to have found was that in the San Francisco Bay area the *average* intelligence of black Americans was lower than the *average* intelligence of whites. Looking at this coolly one ought not to have been more disturbed than by the statement that black Americans have produced more boxing champions than white Americans. But of course few people can look at this coolly, and for reasons that one does not need to be very perceptive to understand. Jensen did not say that any black American you meet you can assume to be less intelligent than any white American – he was talking of averages. And he has said that he is not for 'white supremacy' and segregation. All the same, and assuming that his statistical techniques are sound (a thing I cannot judge), he seems to me open to criticism on several counts.

His findings come from a sample of schools in a single area. He says himself that they might have been different somewhere else. I think it would have been more responsible to have made another such study – say, in Mississippi – before publishing. He must have known that his results would be generalised. I think also that it should have been obvious that there would be generalisation that overlooked the fact that he was talking of averages, translating his work into something like 'Jensen says that whites are more intelligent than blacks', and he might have done more to guard against this.

Secondly, in his famous article in the *Harvard Educational Review*[9] (which is a general review for those interested in education, not a highly technical publication for a limited group of educational psychologists or sociologists) Jensen made a logically illegitimate transition from talk about different racial groups to talk about different groups for teaching and learning. He was trying to make a pedagogical point about those who might not grasp concepts easily but were good at memory work and suggested that these needed a different teaching strategy from the concept-stressing one appropriate to brighter youngsters. But what has this to do with the distinction between black and white Americans that till now he has been talking about? If he was talking only about racial averages there would be some of each race in his learning groups. But to move straight from a racial division to a teaching division in this way was bound to invite misunderstanding.

If Professor Jensen had wished not to be misunderstood and had grasped the nature of the angry dispute that would follow, why did he not begin his Harvard article by saying, quite briefly: (i) that he was not in favour of apartheid or segregated schooling, (ii) that there seems to be a difference in average intelligence as between black and white Americans, and that as this is genetic we may have here a partial explanation of the failure so far of compensatory education for black children, (iii) that he believed that educationally people should be treated as individuals, and irrespective of the colours of their skin and (iv) that to be fair to all individuals we must realise that while measured intelligence is a factor in winning awards in American life there must be an ethical question as to whether this is unjust, on average, to black Americans. He would still have been involved in argument, not least as to what is genetic and what environmental (as one critic said, just being a black American gives you a different psychic environment from being a white) but the grosser misunderstandings would not have occurred.

The best reply to research findings that we doubt is another research study or some equally valid appeal to studied human experience. But what is the layman to do when the research methods are partly those of extreme statistical sophistication? How can a teacher or elected member of a school board or education committee be a skilled and critical judge of these procedures? What's a varimax rotation to him, or he to a varimax rotation? He can only use his layman's commonsense, and if he is against racial discrimination he may react as Jensen will say he didn't expect. But if Jensen wasn't trailing his coat a little (an unworthy suspicion, but there are academics who get a bit wrong-headed even about what they may justly feel to be right) why didn't he see this? I think he has been very intolerantly treated, and nothing can justify that. But I also think that he might have known it would happen. That, he and other research workers might say, is as it may be: it is not their business. I think it is. And not just to save them from unpleasantness, but to further sound discussion leading less to hysteria and more to the truth.

Let me end this chapter by summing up what I have been saying. We clearly need more educational research, and of the strict kind, into matters on which for lack of information we are not yet competent to make sound policy decisions. But research is not the only kind of valid and important educational study. The two other kinds I have mentioned are no substitute for research. But for insight into children's and adults' experience when they are learning, or what they feel when deprived of education, the direct and personal expression of experience imaginatively realised can be of the greatest importance, because it makes these dry bones live. And there is need for a more recognised place for what I have called the policy paper, the paper that bases itself on research but also on considered values and priorities and on what is possible in practice. In short we need more educational research but a clear understanding of what it can and cannot do.

Do we now need, then, research into research? Heaven forbid! Just that clearer understanding of what we are and are not doing that would make so much difference.

Notes and References

Note: The place of publication of books is London unless otherwise stated.

PAGE 12

The quotation is taken from the Goethe volume in the Penguin Poets series, edited by David Luke (1964), who gives the following plain prose translation:

> 'Goats, to the left with you!' the Judge one day will ordain. 'And you, little sheep, stand quietly here on my right!' – Fair enough; but it is to be hoped that he will say one thing more, namely: 'As for you, stand right opposite me, you men of sense!'

CHAPTER 1

1 M. Miles, in R. Hooper (ed.), *The Curriculum: Context, Design and Development* (Edinburgh, Oliver & Boyd and the Open University, 1971).
2 A. Halpin (ed.), *Administrative Theory in Education* (New York, Macmillan, 1967; first edn 1958).
3 D. Lawton, *Class, Culture and the Curriculum* (Routledge & Kegan Paul, 1975).
4 R. Whitfield (ed.), *Discipline of the Curriculum* (McGraw-Hill, 1971).
5 B. Bloom *et al.*, *A Taxonomy of Educational Objectives.* The basic volume is the first, *The Cognitive Domain* (Longmans, 1956).
6 (Paris, Organisation for Economic Development and Co-operation, 1975), *passim* and especially p. 166.
7 M. Macdonald-Ross, 'Behavioural objectives, a critical review', *Instructional Science*, Vol. 2, No. 1 (May 1973; Amsterdam, Elsevier).
8 N. Chomsky, *Language and Mind* (New York, Harcourt Brace Yovanovitch, 1972), pp. 101, 102.
9 S. Moskovitz, 'Behavioural objectives: new ways to fail children', *Young Children* (April 1973; Washington DC).
10 G. Bantock, 'Towards a theory of popular education', in Hooper, op. cit. (reprinted from articles in the *Times Educational Supplement*, 12 and 19 March 1971).
11 P. H. Hirst, *Knowledge and the Curriculum* (Routledge & Kegan Paul, 1974), p. 25.
12 In *Educational Philosophy and Theory*, Vol. 6 (New South Wales University Press, 1974).
13 The examples given in the paper 'The nature and structure of curriculum knowledge', in *Knowledge and the Curriculum*, p. 25, are, if one does not scrutinise them, the most telling ones. 'A moral judgement is not validated in the same way as a mathematical theorem, nor a historical explanation in the same way as a theological proposition.' But if one does scrutinise them, what is their status? The first contrast stands because mathematics is the one study that does have different criteria from the others, not relying on the tests of experience but on internal consistency only. The second falls because, as I explain later, the category of religious propositions as a form of knowledge in the objective sense is open to all kinds of objections. The comments on history are in the essay 'The forms of knowledge revisited' in the same volume (p. 86).
14 Professor Hamlyn, although not satisfied with the Correspondence Theory of Truth as an account of what Truth is, emphasises its important functions: 'If correspondence with fact is not part of the meaning of truth, it does at least seem to be the constituent condition of truth.' ('The correspondence theory of truth, in *Reason*, Vol. 2 of *Education and the Development of Reason*, Routledge & Kegan Paul, 1972, p. 118.) Professor Hirst does not mention this paper though he may have had it in mind. He was one of the three editors of the volume.
15 Hirst, op. cit., pp. 152–64.

16 See Marrou, *History of Education in Antiquity* (Mentor Books, 1964). Homer as the educator of Greece portrayed a style of life related closely to military accomplishments. In Athenian education it was athletic rather than firmly military prowess that was important. With Socrates and the Sophists intelligence began to take precedence over athleticism. In the Hellenic age, with the disappearance of the public role of the citizen in the now superseded city-state, style of life again became the ruling conception, with an increasing emphasis on literature rather than music.

17 In Hooper, op. cit.

18 Quoted in ibid., Introduction to Part II.

19 A. D. C. Peterson, *Arts and Science Sides in the Sixth Form*, report to the Gulbenkian Foundation (Oxford University Department of Education, 1960).

20 What 'pragmatic' means in curriculum reform may be seen in the excellent keynote address given by L. C. Taylor to the Commonwealth Conference on Materials for Learning held in Wellington, New Zealand, in September 1975 (Commonwealth Secretariat, Marlborough House, Pall Mall, London). After noting that many experiments in curriculum had been disappointing because it had not been realised that the new way of learning had all sorts of 'supply' implications, such as physical replanning and retraining of teachers, and after rejecting the 'nauseating jargon' of Bloom, Mr Taylor says that major curricular experiments should be effected a few at a time with full concern for the attendant things without which they cannot succeed. This paper (which could well stand publication in a more accessible form) expresses on the side of practical application exactly the kind of commonsense for which I have been pleading.

CHAPTER 2

Note: The views expressed in this chapter were first formulated in an address I was invited to give at an annual meeting of the Joint Association of Classical Teachers.

1 K. Martin, *Father Figures* (Hutchinson, 1966), Ch. 3.

2 In his essay on 'Education'.

3 *Didaskalos* is the annual publication of the Joint Association of Classical Teachers, published by the Merman Press and edited by John Sharwood Smith, head of the classics department of the London University Institute of Education. In this chapter I am simply giving support to the views of Mr Sharwood Smith and his fellow reformers.

4 F. M. Cornford, *The Republic of Plato* (Oxford, The Clarendon Press, 1941), Preface, p. vi.

CHAPTER 3

1 There is a briefer discussion of technical education and liberal values, with some reference to the views of Aristotle and their adaptation to nineteenth-century England, in my *Education and Contemporary Society* (Watts, 1965), pp. 182–93.

2 Harris Rackham's translation of the *Politics* (Loeb edn, Heinemann, 1932), VIII, 2.

3 A more defensible position was that of Newman, for whom merely useful information was not a sign of being educated. As his editor May Yardley puts it, education was not knowledge but a preparation for knowledge. (May Yardley, ed., *The Idea of a University*, Cambridge, 1931, p. xxiii.)

4 Quoted in B. Colloms, *Charles Kingsley* (Constable, 1975), p. 206.

5 K. Freeman, *Schools of Hellas* (reprinted as No. 38 in the Classics in Education series, Columbia Teachers' College, 1969).

6 L. Stephen, *Life of Sir James Fitzjames Stephen* (Smith Elder, 1895), pp. 80, 81.

7 *Politics* (Loeb edn), VII, 8.

8 D. Newsome, *Godliness and Good Learning* (John Murray, 1961).

9 S. Chase, *Men and Machines* (Jonathan Cape, 1929).

10 Ashby, *Technology in Education* (Wunsch, 1966), Tecknion, Haifa, 1967.

CHAPTER 4

Note: I was generously invited (as a spokesman for the opposition – no one was discourteous enough to say Devil's Advocate) to a conference about religious education in schools held in April 1965. The proceedings were edited by the Rev. Alexander Wedderspoon with the title *Religious Education, 1944–1984* (George Allen & Unwin, 1966). My paper to the conference is printed in this and I have drawn upon it considerably for the purpose of the present chapter.

 1 In England we have a system of public schools, but we feel that we cannot refer to the schools in it as public schools because that term is used, normally with capital letters, for the independent schools whose headmasters are members of the Headmasters' Conference. Again, for publicly owned schools the technical term 'county schools' is not used except in official parlance, and the term 'state schools' is wrong because an LEA is not a state. The United States is free of this confusion: the public school is one that belongs to the public and a private school, one that is in private hands. I think we should follow this same rational usage. So I propose to call the traditionally styled Public Schools 'independent schools' (which they are, though not the only ones). Independent schools in England are to be distinguished both from schools that belong to the public and from private schools that are aided in one degree or another by public funds and are therefore, though not public, also not independent. The right word for schools that belong to the public is obviously 'public schools' and I think we should start using it.
 2 See B. Colloms, *Charles Kingsley* (Constable, 1975), p. 313.
 3 See *The Humanist Newsletter* (British Humanist Association), April 1975.
 4 *Religious Education in the Nursery and Infant Schools* (Christian Institute of Education, 1964), p. 23.

CHAPTER 5

 1 See, for example, P. Hirst, in J. F. Kerr (ed.), *Changing the Curriculum* (University of London Press, 1968), p. 45.
 2 For an account of Colenso and the effect his independent and honest thinking produced, see G. Faber, *Jowett* (Faber, 1957), pp. 317*ff*.
 3 K. Nott, *The Emperor's Clothes* (Heinemann, 1953).
 4 S. Toulmin, *The Place of Reason in Ethics* (CUP, 1950).
 5 J. H. Barnsley, *The Social Reality of Ethics* (Routledge & Kegan Paul, 1972).
 6 J. H. Werkmeister, *Man and his Values* (Lincoln, Nebraska, University of Nebraska, Press, 1967).
 7 P. Souper, *About to Teach* (Routledge & Kegan Paul, 1976). There is an excellent discussion of the need for (and in our rapidly changing civilisation the increasing difficulty of attaining) a secure personal set of values in the first five chapters of W. D. Wall, *Constructive Education for Children* (Harrap, 1975). For the maturing of my views on education – which are not necessarily his – I owe a great deal to my many discussions over the years with Professor Wall.
 8 The teacher's obligations in relation to facts and values are considered in Part Four of the symposium *Philosophers Discuss Education*, ed. S. C. Brown (Macmillan, 1975). Mary Warnock, without going deeply into the difficulty of distinguishing facts from values, makes the commonsense assumption that I have made here, that we can make statements that we term statements of facts and, equally, evaluative statements. But because interpretation enters into presentation from the start, the teacher cannot be just neutral. Indeed, his ability to show his class how he has come to his personal conclusions is part of his educative function. All this is true and Mrs Warnock talks about it in very practical teaching terms.
   I would, however, make two points. Mrs Warnock may be right in saying it is logically impossible and psychologically frustrating for a teacher to say at one and the same time 'This is wrong' and 'But you need not think so'; it is possible

to say 'I think this is wrong and for the following reasons' and 'Others do not think it wrong and these are the reasons they give'. Secondly, the distinction between values and beliefs is important here. On the basic values without which society will be corrupt or break down (such as truth-telling and consideration for others) the teacher cannot be neutral. There are others where good men differ, and these values often cut across differences of belief. Here a teacher should not be afraid to give his own conclusions and say how he has reached them, noting that others take a different view. But with belief-systems the position is not the same. Here the teacher must surely see himself as the trustee of parents of many different kinds of belief and disbelief and in the classroom must refrain from pressing his own belief-system at the expense of others.

CHAPTER 6

1 'Can educationalists agree while philosophers differ?', *Adult Education* (December 1947).
2 *Times Educational Supplement* (23 August 1947).
3 L. Woolf, *Sowing* (Hogarth Press, 1960), pp. 55–8.

CHAPTER 7

Note: I first wrote on this subject in the first part of a paper in *Melbourne Studies in Education, 1968–69*, the paper having been delivered at the preceding Fink Memorial Seminar in the University of Melbourne. I developed my view of the subject, first in a valedictory lecture at the London University Institute of Education and then in a further lecture in the School of Teacher Education in the Canberra College of Advanced Education in 1974.

1 D. D. Raphael (ed.), *Political Theory and the Rights of Man* (Macmillan, 1967).
2 R. H. Fennesey, *Burke, Paine and the Rights of Man* (The Hague, Nijhoff, 1963).
3 In A. de Crespigny and A. Wertheimer, *Contemporary Political Theory* (Nelson, 1971).
4 'Are there any natural rights?', in Quinton (ed.), *Political Philosophy* (OUP, 1967).
5 M. Ginsberg (ed.), *Law and Opinion in England in the Twentieth Century* (Stevens, 1959), in his initial paper.
6 M. Cranston, *What Are Human Rights?* (The Bodley Head, 1973).
7 H. Street, *Freedom, the Individual and the Law* (Penguin, 1967).
8 H. J. McCloskey, in P. J. Frensham (ed.), *Rights and Equality in Australian Education* (Cheshire, 1970).
9 S. I. Benn and R. S. Peters, *Social Principles and the Democratic State* (George Allen & Unwin, 1959), p. 98. Their quotation from Laski is from his Grammar of Politics (5th edn, George Allen & Unwin, 1948), p. 94.

CHAPTER 8

1 W. G. Runciman, *Relative Deprivation and Social Justice* (Pelican Books, 1972), p. 301, quoting R. H. Tawney in R. Hinden (ed.), *The Radical Tradition* (George Allen & Unwin, 1964), Ch. 10.
2 In his article attacking the Federation of British Industries for their hostility to the extension of education (Ch. 4 in Hinden, op. cit.), Tawney again says that one cannot refute their theory of society by argument, but also says that their motives and social policy 'have only to be stated in order to be rejected decisively by the public opinion of the community'. This, I am sure, was his real position.
3 R. H. Tawney, *Equality* (George Allen & Unwin, 1931), p. 109.
4 In A. de Crespigny and A. Wertheimer, *Contemporary Political Theory* (Nelson, 1971).
5 S. I. Benn and R. S. Peters, *Social Principles and the Democratic State* (George Allen & Unwin, 1959), p. iii.

6 S. Hook, *Education for Modern Man* (New York, Knopf, 1963), pp. 36–41.

7 Quoted in G. H. Sabine, *History of Political Theory* (Harrap, 1944), p. 483.

8 See note 6.

9 Runciman, op. cit., pp. 297*ff*.

10 M. Young, *The Rise of the Meritocracy* (Thames & Hudson, 1958).

11 Professor Galbraith made this phrase famous through his book *The Affluent Society* (Boston, Houghton Mifflin, 1958). I owe to one classical friend the information that it was used by Justin Martyr (*c.* 100 to *c.* 165 AD) and to another that Sallust (83–35 BC) used it in his *Catiline* in the accusative form.

12 R. H. Tawney, *Equality* (George Allen & Unwin, 1931), p. 142.

13 Charles Kingsley, both Tory and radical reformer, had a less crude view of equality of opportunity in education. Writing at the time of the Education Bill of 1870, he said:

> If I had my way, I would give the same education to the child of the collier and to the child of the peer. I would see that they were taught the same things, and by the same method. Let them all begin alike, say I. They will be handicapped enough as they go on in life, without our handicapping them in their first race. Whatever stable they come out of, whatever promise they show, let them all train alike and start fair, and let the best colt win.

(B. Colloms, *Charles Kingsley*, Constable, 1975, p. 328.) Mrs Thatcher (if I may continue Kingsley's metaphor) does not seem to have got to the first hurdle in thinking out her concept.

14 Christopher Jencks *et al., Inequality* (New York, Basic Books, 1973), p. 106.

15 In *Perspectives on Education* (Columbia Teachers' College, 1974).

16 M. Arnold, 'Schools and universities on the Continent' (1868), in R. H. Super (ed.), *Prose Works*, Vol. 4 (University of Michigan Press, 1964).

17 Reprinted in Hinden, op. cit., and quoted in Willem van der Eyken (ed.), *Education, the Child and Society* (Penguin, 1973).

CHAPTER 10

Note: This chapter, except for the first paragraph, appeared as a paper in the *Oxford Review of Education*, Vol. I, No. 3 (1975). Some of the latter part derives from a paper I read on 'The setting of educational research', at the annual meeting of the National Foundation for Educational Research in 1971.

1 Michael Joseph, 1960; Penguin, 1962.

2 R. Hoggart, *The Uses of Literacy* (Chatto & Windus, 1957; Penguin, 1958).

3 B. Jackson and D. Marsdon, *Education and the Working Class* (Routledge & Kegan Paul, 1952; Penguin, 1956); and *Working Class Community* (Routledge & Kegan Paul, 1968; Penguin, 1972).

4 G. Myrdal, *Value in Social Theory* (Routledge & Kegan Paul, 1958).

5 *15 to 18*, report of the Central Advisory Council, England (HMSO, 1959).

6 *Higher Education*, report of the Committee appointed by the prime minister (HMSO, 1963).

7 S. Hilsum and B. S. Cane, *The Teacher's Day* (NFER, 1971).

8 P. Coombs, *The World Education Crisis*, a Systems Analysis (OUP, 1968).

9 *Harvard Educational Review*, Vol. 39, No. 1 (1969).

Index

Index